INTERPRETING THE INTERPRETERS:

STRATEGIES FOR A SCIENCE OF CONSTRUING PEOPLE

INTERPRETING THE INTERPRETERS

Linda L. Viney
Chairman, Dept. of Psychology
The University of Wollongong
Australia

ROBERT E. KRIEGER PUBLISHING COMPANY
MALABAR, FLORIDA
1987

Original Edition 1987

Printed and Published by
ROBERT E. KRIEGER PUBLISHING COMPANY, INC.
KRIEGER DRIVE
MALABAR, FLORIDA 32950

Copyright © 1987 by Robert E. Krieger Publishing Co., Inc.

Printed in the United States of America

Library of Congress Cataloging-in-Publication Data

Viney, Linda L.
    Interpreting the Interpreters.

    Includes bibliographies.
    1. Personal construct theory—Research—Evaluation. I. Title.
BF698.9.P47V56   1987   155.2   86-7180
ISBN 0-89874-932-8

10 9 8 7 6 5 4 3 2

CONTENTS

262259

PREFACE

Many of the ideas expressed in this book had their genesis almost a decade ago, when I was fortunate to have a full year of sabbatical leave from my university. During that period I stepped out of a self-regenerating cycle of data collection to think seriously about my role as a research psychologist. My self-questioning at that time has become a habit which I now hope to pass on to other researchers. At the beginning of each chapter I have therefore placed a set of questions which each psychologist or student of psychology can ask of himself or herself. At the end of each chapter is a list of the references which I have found useful.

The issues I have raised include the assumptions that we, as psychologists, make about ourselves and our subject matter (Chapter 1) and their implications for the models of data collection we use (Chapter 2). These implications are considered in relation to the roles of both subject (Chapter 3) and experimenter (Chapter 4) and the relationships between them when data are collected (Chapter 5). Appropriate tools for such data collection are examined (Chapter 6), together with strategies for their use in a range of areas of psychology (Chapter 7).

My colleagues have contributed much by discussion of these methodological issues. But my thanks must also be extended to the senior undergraduate and graduate students at Macquarie University and the University of Wollongong whose interest in and concern for these issues has challenged me to write about them.

CHAPTER 1

PEOPLE AS CONSTRUERS

2

What assumptions do we make about the people whom we study?

What assumptions do we make about ourselves as psychologists?

Can we gain access to the experience of another person?

How can we relate experience to behaviour?

Subjective and objective: Are they compatible perspectives for psychologists?

Many psychologists have argued that it is our current tools of data collection that determine what we study, rather than the nature of our subject matter (Giorgi, 1970; Harré, 1979; Herzog, 1979; Koch, 1981; Hetherington, 1983). They have also claimed that the psychology which has resulted presents a limited view of the person who should be the centre of our activities. I believe that knowledge is created by people (Bridgman, 1959; van Kaam, 1966) and that it is a function of our interpretations (Polyani, 1958; Cassirer, 1967). It is for these reasons that I have selected personal construct psychology and other sociophenomenological approaches to overcome some of these limitations.

Personal Construct Psychology

The basic postulate of personal construct psychology takes this form: "A person's processes are psychologically channelized by the ways in which he or she anticipates events." (Kelly, 1955, p.467). People try to anticipate, not passively accept, what is going to happen to them. They use this information to decide what they do and when they do it (Bannister & Fransella, 1985). Inherent in this postulate is the fanciful but productive notion of people as scientists. People are like scientists in constantly seeking to achieve a better understanding of their world. Their constructs or hypotheses help them to do this. This personal construct model presents them as scientists even to the extent of formulating hypotheses, checking them out against data, and reformulating them as necessary. Hypotheses are, after all, only anticipatory interpretations (Strasser, 1963).

If this assumption about hypothesis testing can be made about people in general, then it can be made about both the experimenters and the subjects in any psychological study. This statement can be made because of another tenet of personal construct psychology. Approaches to humanity should be reflexive. They should apply to psychologists as well as to their focus of study, to subjects as well as to objects. This implies a science of psychology which is both by and about construing or interpreting people.

Kelly's picture of psychologists is of fundamentally active people ascribing meaning to their worlds, that is, to their perceptions of their environment and of the people in it. There will, inevitably, be assumptions made in those searches for meaning. In this regard Kelly has applied at least two of the corollaries of his postulate: the choice corollary and the experience corollary. The first states that "a person chooses for himself (or herself) that alternative . . . through which he/she anticipates the greater possibility for extension and definition of his/her system" (1955, p.64). Psychologists are, therefore, seen as selecting among any set of alternatives open to them those which they believe will most broaden and clarify the constructs through which they view the world. These constructs also change as a function of experience, because people's construct systems vary as they "successively construe the replication of events" (1955, p.72). Psychological researchers, then, can be flexible in their use of constructs. They can choose those which give them the best opportunity for contact with the phenomena they study.

Personal construct psychology is essentially a phenomenological approach. Kelly, himself, specifically disclaimed taking such a position (1969). He was not, however, entirely accurate in his understanding of phenomenology;

no more so, at any rate, than many American psychologists of his day. It is clear that, for Kelly, experience holds the key for psychology. Many of his ideas are similar to those proposed independently by the sociophenomenologist, Schütz, whose approach is described later in this chapter (Holland, 1970). The importance which Kelly gives to people's flexibility in interpreting the events they experience, marks him as a phenomenologist. Further, his rejection of classifactory systems in psychology, and of the stick-and-carrot concepts of motivation, indicate that he was trying to look at human experience without developing misleading interpretations of it. This is the approach of phenomenology.

Kelly's view of people suggests a partial solution to our lack of awareness of our own assumptions or interpretations when, as psychologists, we study people. It takes the phenomenological position of a multiplicity of perspectives, and has been described by Kelly as "constructive alternativism". Constructive alternativism implies that any collection of data may be usefully viewed from any number of different perspectives, each valid in its turn. This idea, too, has been developed by Schütz (1953), as well as by a number of philosophers of science (Feigl, 1959; Feyerbend, 1968; Goodman, 1978). For all of these writers, these interpretations or assumptions have become friends to be aware of, and not troublesome imponderables to be hidden or ignored.

We psychologists have at times avoided a close examination of the assumptions of our discipline (Wicker, 1985). This avoidance has arisen, presumably, out of fear of being overwhelmed by the many alternatives available. The constructs of, say, psychoanalysis or behaviourism, are not considered to be invalid by constructive alternativism. They provide viable alternative interpretations of the data which are available. Some psychological assumptions may have been distorting our understanding of those data. The use of the methods of the sciences of the physical world in psychology has sometimes led to such distortion (Binswanger, 1941). The solution to this problem has been said to be the formulation of a human science, a science which has at its core an adequate model of humanity (Giorgi, 1971).

This human science has been concerned with the establishment of essential structures or patterns of experience through the rejection of a priori interpretations. Personal construct psychology, however, directs our attention to those interpretations. Only three such distorting sets of interpretations are noted here. The first is the mechanistic model of people. This endows them with the characteristics of machines but little else (Joynson, 1974). The second is the concept of cause as the sole explanatory device. This model focusses on theoretical factors outside the person to the exclusion of the links between cause and effect within the person, his or her history and social context (Harré & Secord, 1972; Bhaskar, 1975). The third consists of the androcentric model of people which has been revealed by the feminist critique of psychology (Acker, Barry & Esseveld, 1983; Unger, 1983; Lott, 1985). When people become scientists they start to act like scientists, making the interpretations which are currently part and parcel of that social role (Schütz, 1945; Latour & Woolgar, 1979). This is undoubtedly true of contemporary psychologists (Salmon, 1978). Yet there are many other sets of interpretations available to them.

"In its early, naive stage, scientists . . . imagined that we could observe things in themselves, as they would behave in our absence . . . Now when scientists reach the end of their analyses they cannot tell with any certainty whether the structure they have made is the essence of the matter they are studying, or a reflection of their own thought" (Teilhard de Chardin, 1959, p.32). Teilhard de Chardin's own science was geology, but this general statement is valid for psychologists as scientists as well. Reflection completely without personal bias is not possible (Holland, 1970). Yet we often are not even aware of our own constructs or of their effects. If we can investigate with fewer a priori interpretations, then psychology may be the better for it. If we can also remember that it is through many perspectives that all phenomena are known, then psychology may have a brighter future.

Other Phenomenological Approaches

The main aim of phenomenology has been to clarify human experience. Perception has therefore been described as central for phenomenology (Sallis, 1973). Perception is not, however, the perception which we define narrowly when we associate it with cognition. It is the interpretation, based on emotion as well as cognition, of personal construct psychology (McCoy, 1977). It is not about facts. It is about meaning, perceived meaning, personal meaning, and social meaning (Bhaskar, 1975; Gergen, 1985). It is about invention (Watzlawick, 1984). People construe their perceived worlds so that they take on specific meanings. Qualitative analyses of these meanings may be as important as the quantitative assessments which we tend to favour (Glaser & Strauss, 1967; Patton, 1980). Each subject participating in psychological research may be seen as endowing the enquiry with private meanings and interpretations, that is, with his or her own constructs, as well as with commonly shared constructs. So, too, does each experimenter.

Knowledge about these construed worlds or people can provide much valuable information for psychologists (Taylor, 1973). Development of such knowledge seems to proceed mainly by way of description. The phenomenological approach requires a more demanding form of description than is usual. It is one which can entail rejecting a priori interpretations, that is, approaching phenomena without presuppositions (Alexander, 1970). Even the basic belief in the very existence of the object of study can be suspended (Gurwitsch, 1954). The reductive approach, or bracketing of asumptions, is made in order to discover how knowledge of the world came about (Husserl, 1900). This question is not one with which psychologists need concern themselves now. We must, however, be concerned with subjectivity. "The subjective realm is . . . functioning in all experiencing, all thinking, all life, thus everywhere inseparably involved" (Husserl, 1970, p.112). A brief sketch of the emergence of the phenomenological approach (owing much to the work of Spiegelberg, 1969; 1972) may now be helpful.

Phenomenology was the product of the philosopher Husserl, who was much influenced by the work of Hume (1740). Hume had shaken the foundations of the science of his contemporaries by challenging the central explanatory role they had given to causality. Kant (1781; 1934), too, influenced Husserl's approach, with his distinction between the appearance of things (phenomena) and the things themselves. Husserl was impressed also by Brentano's (1870;

1955) concept of intentionality which takes the position that all thoughts are related to objects. It was on these bases that he advocated a science which recognized subjectivity as the ground of all objectivities (Husserl, 1969; Greenway, 1982). In his Encyclopaedia Britannica article (translated by Palmer, 1971), Husserl (1927) strongly advocated a phenomenological psychology, which he distinguished from traditional psychology. The latter he saw as the study of psychological beings in the context of the psychophysiological organism. For phenomenological psychology he reserved the study of psychological beings in their subjective aspects alone. Both psychologies may be being achieved today, with phenomenological psychology giving rise to our current cognitive science (Dreyfus, 1982). The question which is of concern is whether the latter has anything to offer the former? Do traditional and phenomenological psychologies provide competing or complementary views of humanity?

The answer to this question depends, to a large extent, on whether implementation of ideas stemming from the phenomenological approach can be successfully achieved. The chief method of phenomenology is reflection, an act by which attention is turned to experience (Spiegelberg, 1970). The simplest form of reflection is descriptive phenomenology. This involves a direct exploration of the experienced world. It results in a presentation of experienced phenomena with as few interpretations or constructs as possible. Yet if I relate to an object in my experienced world, I inevitably take a position in relation to that object. That is to say, I construe it. That no reflection or experience is completely without interpretation is basic to the hermeneutic phenomenology of Heidegger (1927; 1962). Interpretive approaches stemming from his work are now being advocated in the reevaluation of the philosophy of the social sciences (Hookway & Pettit, 1978; Rabinow & Sullivan, 1979), as critical social theory (Marsh, 1985) and as feminist critique (Bowles, 1984), as well as in psychology (Packer, 1985).

It is this phenomenological approach which has led personal construct psychologists to make some more fundamental queries. Is a psychological science of the private, subjective interpretations of construing people as viable as our traditional science of distanced, alienated beings has proved to be? Can we isolate structures of experience which are objective in the sense of being agreed upon by different people (Popper, 1959)? And, if we can, will they have bearing on the findings of that traditional psychology? Your answers, and mine, are determined by the definitions of science which we choose to support. It is noteworthy, for example, that this definition of objectivity as subjective agreement is essentially a phenomenological criterion. If science is seen as having for its goal intersubjectively agreed upon knowledge gained in a rigorous and consistent manner, an affirmative answer seems possible. If, on the other hand, the science of psychology is limited to the methodologies of the physical sciences - the sciences which do not focus on construing people - then a negative answer is more likely.

People as Construers

It was at the climax of a careful examination of the assumptions which might underlie a psychology of personality, that this view of people as construers was derived. "Man meets experience with meaningful conceptions of basic premises and fashions it at least as much as experience fashions him" (Rychlak,

1970, p.470). It is this picture of people as the active interpreters of their worlds, inherent in personal construct psychology, which makes it important to examine our own interpretations (Grene, 1967). While the number of psychologists claiming to support this view is legion, the extent to which it has influenced the research of psychologists has not been great. My recent survey of the current volumes of leading journals in the fields of physiological psychology, perception and cognition, learning, personality and social psychology (to be described in more detail in Chapter 6) has indicated that research psychologists rarely appear to conceive of their so-called subjects as construing people. Nor, more surprisingly, do they recall that the same assumption may be made about their experimenters. This is surprising because these experimenters are often the research psychologists themselves. It appears that the concept of reflexivity is not accepted by them.

Some aspects of my assumption that people are active construers or interpreters need to be drawn out more fully. What I am doing now, in the phenomenological tradition, is examining my own interpretations, and not trying to foist them on others. The reader should examine his or her own interpretations. Later, in Chapters 3, 4, and 5, I shall examine the implications that my interpretations can have for psychological research.

What does it mean, then, when experimenters view their subjects as "active"? People may be viewed as the source of acts. This implies that they are active rather than reactive and not simply mindless responders to stimuli, as the neobehaviourists now agree (Bandura, 1977; Mischel, 1977). Subjects of psychological research can act, as well as react, with their experimenters. This capacity for action also implies that people are makers of choices, even aware makers of choices. This is a position also compatible with the general phenomenological approach (Zaner, 1970) and with that of personal construct psychology in particular. Shotter (1975) has illuminated the effects of this construed choice for traditional scientific determinism by the use of a lesson from the fifteenth-century humanist, Pico della Mirandola. "Consider," said della Mirandola, in effect, "how we might view the world if we thought our God had not created Adam and Eve in his own image, but had actually offered them a choice of form." This is, indeed, a radical idea!

People are assumed not only to experience but to construe their experience (Giddens, 1977; Buss, 1978). People carve out structures or meanings within experience (Shepherd & Watson, 1982). People symbolize, synthesize and explore (Hampden-Turner, 1971). People "ascribe purpose and meaning, even in the absence of purpose and meaning" (Orne, 1962, p.780). These assumptions have led to the recognition of the role of the demand characteristics of the data collection situation for the subjects of psychological research. The interpretations which people choose may be a function, not only of their current situation as they perceive it, but also of their past experiences and future goals. These interpretations are accessible to psychologists through a variety of tools. One example is the Role Construct Repertory Technique (Kelly, 1955). This technique is examined in some detail in Chapter 6.

Rocks and plants do not, so far as I can tell, construe or interpret. Another way in which people are different from the objects of other sciences is in their capacity for reflection, their ability to know that they are aware of things (Roche,

1973). Each person is particularly aware of himself or herself, and of that self as knower. It is noteworthy that at least one attempt to devise a more viable social psychology has assumed that people follow rules and that they know that they do (Harré, 1971). Personal construct psychology takes this one step further. People are regarded as capable of saying what they are up to. This is an important development in our view of the relationship between experience and behaviour. It also assumes people to be capable of reflecting on their experiences.

One of the main questions which we must deal with is about the forms that the relationship between the subjectively construed experience of people and their observed behaviour may take. The latter is directly available only to the observer, the psychologist, through his or her senses. The former, in contrast, is perceived directly only by the individual involved and so is only indirectly available to the psychologist (Quill, 1972). Both construed experience and observed behaviour are important for psychology (Quattrone, 1985).

What we need for data collection is a combination of observation (of behaviour) and description (of personal constructs or interpretations) (Campbell, 1969). That these objective and subjective perspectives complement one another is apparent in this example of learning which was used to introduce American psychologists to phenomenological concepts (Snygg, 1941). Let us imagine, firstly, that we are watching a small boy learn how to do a task, say, solve a puzzle. From our external view, that task remains the same during the learning period, but the responses of the child change as he successfully solves his puzzle. We are, then, likely to ascribe the process of change to the learner. From the second perspective, the viewpoint of the active child, he himself is unchanged during learning. It is the perceived nature of the task which changes. Different interpretations, or alternative constructions, are possible.

How have psychologists related observed behaviour and construed experience to date? A significant number of them view construed experience as a determinant of observed behaviour. "All behaviour, without exception, is completely determined by, and pertinent to, the perceptual field of the behaving organism" (Combs & Snygg, 1959, p.20). This statement provides an explicit statement of this view. People's constructs are seen by some as the determinant, not a determinant, of their behaviour (Apter, 1982). Other psychologists (Rickard, 1971) view observed behaviour as a determinant of construed experience. Both of these interpretations, which maintain one-way causation in the relationship between experience and behaviour, appear to have had a limiting rather than an enabling effect on psychological research.

The position of personal construct psychology in regard to their relationship is more complex. It maintains that the behaviour of people can best be understood in terms of their interpretations of their worlds, which in turn are a function of their behaviour and so on. We cannot, then, arrive at adequate explanations of behaviour until we take the constructs of the behavers into account (Harré, 1978). Behaviour and experience are part of a total, overriding Gestalt, which consists of a person involved in the situation (Giorgi, 1971). The Gestalt is sometimes difficult to bring into focus. The reciprocal nature of the relationship between construed experience and observed behaviour has been described in this way. What I call experience is your behaviour behaved by you. What I call behaviour is your experience behaved by me. Conversely, your experience is my behaviour behaved by me, while your behaviour is my

experience behaved by you (Romanyshyn, 1975). This is itself a matter of

interpretation. It distinguishes the actor's perspective on events from that of the

observer. It also reminds us that psychology is about and even part of a social

world. Psychology involves a construed world in which some constructs are

shared. This world also involves the constant give and take of interpersonal

interaction.

Construing the Social World

Psychology is embedded in the social world in part because of the topic it

has chosen for itself: the person. This means that any collection by a

psychologist (a person) of psychological data (from another person) must involve

interaction between construing people. In the simplest of possible paradigms,

there is interpersonal interaction between the experimenter and the subject, the

tester and the client and the questionnaire user and the respondent. This

involves two-way interaction between people, all with their own interpretations of

their situation and capacity to act and react. Psychologists are trying to construe

the construing processes of another. They are trying to interpret the interpreted

world of the other. When that occurs the psychologist comes to "play a role in a

social process involving the other person" (Kelly, 1955, p.95).

Schütz is more helpful to us than Kelly here, since he has concerned

himself both with how people interact and what this implies for the social

sciences. Schütz's contribution is actually more methodological than theoretical

(Thomason, 1982). He has maintained that, when people act, their behaviour is directed towards an end. It involves a plan. Otherwise it is simply expressive behaviour. The purpose of their actions constitutes their meaning. Motives may be "in-order-to" motives leading to the achievement of interim goals. Alternatively, they may be "because" motives, when the situation they are in appears to demand an outcome. These meanings, of course, are available only through interpretations of experience. So we must study those interpretations. Schütz (1945) has quoted William James in this regard: "Each world while it is attended to is real after its own fashion; only the reality lapses with the attention."

The social world of each individual is assumed to coexist with him or her. Other people are conceived of as construing just as each construes himself or herself. If they share a situation with another, that other person is assumed to be construing that situation in ways similar to their own. They interpret the experience of others by observing their expressive behaviour and guessing at their motives by imagining themselves to be behaving in those ways. They also interpret the behaviour of others through their communicative acts. The expression of meaning is assumed by Schütz to be the "in-order-to" motive for a communicative act. Communication often takes place through symbols. This conceptualisation is similar to that of Mead and the symbolic interactionists, whose contribution to this interpretation of the interpreters will be considered in Chapter 2.

Interpersonal interaction is normally a spontaneous activity which springs from construed experience and is directed towards another experiencing self (Schütz, 1967). It is other-orientated. The "in-order-to" motive is to bring about certain experiences for the other person. In a fully functioning face-to-face interaction there is mutual orientation. I am aware that you are aware that I am aware . . . and so it goes on. As I understand your plan it becomes part of my definition of the situation that we are in. If I want our relationship to continue, your plan must become my motive for my own action. And as I communicate with you, my in-order-to motive will become your "because" motive and your "in-order-to" motive will become my "because" motive. This interplay of motives is essential if we are to know whether we share the same meanings. There is a sharing of worlds with their interpretations and values as well as motives. There is a sharing of constructs.

Of course, not all interpersonal relationships involve such mutual orientation. Observation, a tool of many psychologists, does not. Behaviours, not purposeful actions, are observed. The constructs which provide a context for these behaviours are available only indirectly. I can suggest much from observing you. I can do so by imaginatively putting myself in your place, by using knowledge from our other interactions in which there was an interplay of motives and by inferring your "in-order-to" motive from your behaviour. But if we do not have a mutual orientation as reflective interpreters of our experience, I can never be sure that I understand your constructs.

Some assumptions of this kind, involving intersubjective sharing of interpretations, seem to me to be essential for a science of construing people. They can be expressed as follows.

1. Other people exist.

2. They are able to retain their interpretations of their experience in memory.

3. They can communicate their interpretations in statements.

4. Their statements are comprehensible to others.

These assumptions about humanity underlie most of our current data collection models, whether we can defend them or not. Unless psychological data come from people who are trying to communicate, they will not be amenable to meaningful interpretation. Psychology needs "a phenomenology of the other one" (Campbell, 1969, p.66).

The Personal Construct Perspective

In this chapter I have examined some of the implications of personal construct psychology for psychological research, especially the importance of the interpretation of experience. How some parts of the private worlds of people are accessible through phenomenological reflection has been described. Concern has been raised about the effects of unexamined interpretations on psychology. I have used the personal construct view of people as scientists and, reflexively, of scientists as construing people, to demonstrate a way of functioning for psychologists which is relatively flexible and tolerant of other perspectives and so of different interpretations.

I then set out to examine some of my own interpretations. One of these concerned people as construers. It was noted that this assumption, a construct in itself, involved a view of people as actors and choosers, as creators of meaning, as reflective knowers and knowing that they know. This view is directly applicable to both the experimenters and the subjects of psychological research. These are interpretations that many psychologists make for most of their fellow human beings but not about those involved in psychological research. They, in turn, invoked the difficult problem of how to conceptualise the relationship between construed experience and observed behaviour. It seemed most profitable to regard both experience and behaviour as a part of a total interpretation of the person. Finally, the construed social world was examined. The social world is important to psychology because the collection of psychological data by a psychologist is an interpersonal event. Schütz's description of such an event and of the people who participate in it was considered. A psychology of construing people is created by people about people who are active interpreting beings. It is also inherently interpersonal in nature.

In the rest of this book I shall consider issues relevant to a science of construing people. The resulting psychology will not be of interest to psychologists who are not concerned with people as construers. It will have as its field of research human experience and behaviour. It will be governed by a set of principles for building up its body of knowledge which assume both psychologists and their subject matter to be interpreters. I shall heed the warning that the findings of such a science must be compatible with both those principles and our everyday, common sense experiences (Wagner, 1970). This science of interpretation will deal with meanings (Taylor, 1973). Psychologists who tread this path with me will need considerable self-knowledge, freedom from illusion and a sense of error. It has been argued that social scientists can do their job well only if they are blind to their role (Cole, 1980). However, "nothing is more subjective than objectivity blind to its subjectivity" (Laing, 1982, p.12).

Now I want to reflect on some aspects of psychological research, examining in Chapter 2 the models of data collection currently in use. Constructs from symbolic interactionism, a sociophenomenological approach similar to that of Schütz, enable such models to be defined. What happens when we begin to regard the human subjects of psychological experiments as construing people is then examined in Chapter 3. And what are the implications of this assumption when it is made about psychological experimenters? Some of the answers to this question are to be found in Chapter 4. Psychological research is, I have maintained, an essentially intersubjective pursuit. Chapter 5 contains an examination of some of the implications of this position. Psychology is based on interactions between subject and experimenter, research participant and researcher. But it is more than this. It is an approach to people by people, and a system of constructs about how this might best be carried out. In Chapter 6, I have therefore examined some of the data collection tools available to us and evaluated their appropriateness. Finally, in Chapter 7, I have made some suggestions about data collection for a science of psychology which is by and about construing people.

References

Acker, J., Barry, K. & Esseveld, J. (1983). Objectivity and truth: Problems in doing feminist research. Women's Studies International Forum, 4, 423-435.

Alexander, I.W. (1970). What is phenomenology? Journal of British Society for Phenomenology, 1, 3.

Apter, M.S. (1982). The experience of motivation. London: Academic Press.

Bandura, A. (1977). Self efficacy: Toward a unifying theory of behaviour change. Psychological Review, 84, 191-215.

Bannister, D. & Fransella, F. (1985). Inquiring man. 3rd ed. Beckenham: Croom Helm.

Bhaskar, R. (1975). A realist theory of science. Leeds, England: Leeds Books.

Binswanger, L. (1941). On the relationship between Husserl's phenomenology and psychological insight. Philosophy and Phenomenological Research, 2, 199-210.

Bowles, G. (1984). The use of hermeneutics for feminist scholarship. Women's Studies International Forum, 7, 185-188.

Brentano, F. (1870;1955). Psychology from the empirical standpoint. Hamburg: Meiher.

Bridgman, P.N. (1959). The way things are. Cambridge, Mass.: Harvard University Press.

Buss, A.H. (1978). The structure of psychological revolutions. Journal of the History of the Behavioural Sciences, 14, 57-64.

Campbell, D.T. (1969). A phenomenology of the other one: Corrigible, hypothetical, critical. In T. Mischel (Ed.) Human action: Conceptual and theoretical issues (pp.41-69). New York: Academic Press.

Cassirer, E. (1967). Essay on man. New Haven: Yale University Press.

Cole, S. (1980). The sociological method. Chicago: Rand-McNally.

Combs, A.W. & Snygg, D. (1959). Individual behaviour. New York: Harper & Row.

Dreyfus, H.L. (Ed.) (1982). Husserl, intentionality and cognitive science. Cambridge, Mass.: Bradford/MIT Press.

Feigl, H. (1959). Philosophical embarrassments of psychology. American Psychologist, 14, 115-128.

Feyerbend, P. (1968). How to be a good empiricist. In P.H. Midditch (Ed.) Philosophy of science (pp.12-39). Oxford: Oxford University Press.

Gergen, K.J. (1985). The social constructionist movement in modern psychology. American Psychologist, 40, 266-275.

Giddens, A. (1977). Studies in social and political theory. New York: Basic Books.

Giorgi, A. (1970). Psychology as a human science: A phenomenologically-based approach. New York: Harper & Row.

Giorgi, A. (1971). The experience of the subject as a source of data in a psychological experiment. In A. Giorgi, W.F. Fischer & R. Von Eckartsberg (Eds.) Duquesne Studies in Phenomenological Psychology. Pittsburgh, Pa.: Duquesne University Press, 1, 50-57.

Glaser, B. & Strauss, A.L. (1967). The discovery of grounded theory: Strategies for qualitative research. Chicago: Aldine-Atherton.

Goodman, G. (1978). Ways of world making. New York: Harvester.

Greenway, P. (1982). The methodological implications of phenomenological assumptions in humanistic psychology. Australian Journal of Psychology, 34, 231-237.

Grene, M. (1967). Straus' phenomenological psychology. Revue Metaphysique, 21, 94-123.

Gurwitsch, A. (1954). The phenomenological and the psychological approach to consciousness. Philosophy and Phenomenological Research, 15, 303-319.

Hampden-Turner, C. (1971). Radical man: The process of psychosocial development. London: Duckworth.

Harré, R. (1971). Joynson's dilemma. Bulletin of the British Psychological Society, 214, 115-119.

Harré, R. (1978). Accounts, actions and meanings - the practice of participatory psychology. In M. Brenner, P. Marsh & L.M. Brenner (Eds.) Contexts of method (pp.35-36). London: Croom Helm.

Harré, R. (1979). Social being: A theory for social psychology. Oxford: Blackwell.

Harré, R. & Secord, P.T. (1972). The explanation of social behaviour. Oxford: Blackwell.

Heidegger, M. (1962). Being and time. New York: Harper & Row.

Herzog, W. (1979). The critique of objectivism in psychology. Zeitschrift für Psychoanalyse und ihre Anirendungen, 31, 243-264.

Hetherington, R. (1983). Sacred cows and white elephants. Bulletin of the British Psychological Society, 36, 273-280.

Holland, R. (1970). George Kelly: Constructive innocent and reluctant existentialist. In D. Bannister (Ed.) Perspectives in personal construct theory (pp.111-132). London: Academic Press.

Hookway, C. & Pettit, P. (Eds.) (1978). Action and interpretation: Studies in the

philosophy of the social sciences. Cambridge, England: Cambridge

University Press.

Hume, D. (1740; 1928). On human nature. Oxford: Clarendon Press.

Husserl, E. (1900). Logical investigations. Halle: Niemeyer.

Husserl, E. (1927). Phenomenology. Encyclopaedia Britannica, 14(17),

699-702.

Husserl, E. (1969). Cartesian meditations. The Hague: Martinus Nijhoff.

Husserl, E. (1970). The crisis of European sciences and transcendental

phenomenology. Evanston, Ill.: Northwestern University Press.

Joynson, R.B. (1974). Psychology and common sense. London: Routledge &

Kegan Paul.

Kant, E. (1781; 1934). Critique of pure reason. London: Macmillan.

Kelly, G.A. (1955). The psychology of personal constructs. New York: Norton.

Kelly, G.A. (1969). Ontological acceleration. In B. Maher (Ed.) Clinical

psychology and personality: The selected papers of George Kelly

(pp.76-45). New York: Wiley.

Koch, S. (1981). The nature and limits of psychological knowledge. American

Psychologist, 36, 257-269.

Laing, R.D. (1982). The voice of experience. Middlesex: Penguin.

Latour, B. & Woolgar, S. (1979). Laboratory life: The social construction of

scientific facts. Beverly Hills: Sage.

Lott, B. (1985). The potential enrichment of social/personality psychology through feminist research and vice versa. American Psychologist, 40, 155-164.

McCoy, M.M. (1977). A reconstruction of emotion. In D. Bannister (Eds.) New perspectives in personal construct theory (pp.142-154). London: Academic Press.

Marsh, J.L. (1985). Dialectical phenomenology as critical social theory. Journal of the British Society for Phenomenology, 16, 177-193.

Mischel, W. (1977). On the future of personality assessment. American Psychologist, 32, 246-254.

Orne, M.T. (1962). On the social psychology of the psychological experiment with particular reference to demand characteristics and their implications. American Psychologist, 17, 776-783.

Packer, M.J. (1985). Hermeneutic inquiry in the study of human conduct. American Psychologist, 40, 1081-1093.

Palmer, R.E. (1971). "Phenomenology," Edmund Husserl's article for the Encyclopaedia Britannica: A new complete translation. Journal of the British Society for Phenomenology, 2, 77-90.

Patton, M.Q. (1980). Qualitative evaluation methods. London: Sage.

Polyani, M. (1958). Personal knowledge. Chicago: University Press.

Popper. K.R. (1959). The logic of scientific discovery. New York: Basic Books.

Quattrone, G.A. (1985). On the congruity between internal states and actions. Psychological Bulletin, 98, 3-40.

Quill, W.G. (1972). Subjective psychology. New York: Spartan Books.

Rabinow, P. & Sullivan, W.M. (1979). Interpretive social science: A reader. Berkeley: University of California Press.

Rickard, H.C. (Ed.) (1971). Behaviour intervention in human problems. New York: Pergamon.

Roche, M. (1973). Phenomenology, language and the social sciences. Boston: Routledge & Kegan Paul.

Romanyshyn, R.D. (1975). Behaviour, experience and expression: The phenomenon of nostalgia. APA Convention, Chicago.

Rychlak, J.F. (1970). The human person in modern psychological science. British Journal of Medical Psychology, 43, 233-240.

Sallis, J. (1973). Phenomenology and the return to the beginning. Pittsburgh, Pa.: Duquesne University Press.

Salmon, P. (1978). Doing psychological research. In F. Fransella (Ed.), Personal construct psychology 1977. London: Academic Press, 35-44.

Schütz, A. (1945). On multiple realities. Philosophy and Phenomenological Research, 5, 533-576.

Schütz, A. (1953). Common sense and scientific enterprise. Philosophy and Phenomenological Research, 14, 1-38.

Schütz, A. (1967). The phenomenology of the social world. Chicago: Northwestern University Press.

Shepherd, E. & Watson, J.P. (Eds.) (1982). Personal meanings. Chichester Wiley.

Shotter, J. (1975). Images of man in psychological research. London: Methuen.

Snygg, D. (1941). The need for a phenomenological system of psychology. Psychological Review, 48, 404-424.

Spiegelberg, H. (1969). The phenomenological movement: A historical introduction. The Hague: Martinus Nijhoff.

Spiegelberg, H. (1970). On some human uses of phenomenology. In F.J. Smith. (Ed.) Phenomenology in perspective (pp.36-46). The Hague: Martinus Nijhoff.

Spiegelberg, H. (1972). Phenomenology in psychology and psychiatry. Evanston, Ill.: Northwestern University Press.

Strasser, S. (1963). Phenomenology and the human sciences. Pittsburgh, Pa.: Duquesne University Press.

Taylor, C. (1973) Interpretation and the sciences of man. In D. Carr and S. Casey (Eds.) Explanations in phenomenology (pp.47-101). The Hague: Martinus Nijhoff.

Teilhard de Chardin, P. (1959). The phenomenon of man. New York: Harper and Row.

Thomason, B. (1982). Making sense of reification. London: Macmillan.

Unger, R.K. (1983). Through the looking glass: No wonderland yet! (The reciprocal relationship between methodology and modes of reality). Psychology of Women Quarterly, 8, 9-32.

VanKaam, A. (1966). Existential foundations in psychology. Pittsburgh, Pa.: Duquesne University Press.

28

Wagner, H.R. (Ed.) (1970). Alfred Schütz on phenomenology and social relations. Chicago: University of Chicago Press.

Watzlawick, P. (1984). The invented reality: How do we know what we believe we know. New York: Wiley.

Wicker, A.W. (1985). Getting out of our conceptual ruts. American Psychologist, 40, 1094-1103.

Zaner, R.M. (1970). The way of phenomenology. New York: Pegasus.

CHAPTER 2

SOME MODELS OF DATA COLLECTION IN PSYCHOLOGY

Do our data collection models determine the research questions we pursue?

Do we assume that the subjects of psychological enquiries are passively cooperative?

Do we assume that the experimenters of psychological enquiries are ineffectual?

Do we take the capacities of subjects and experimenters for reflection into account?

Do we recognise the interpersonal nature of the data collection interaction?

The symbolic interactionist approach (Mead, 1962) is another sociophenomenological approach which holds many interpretations in common with personal construct psychology. It has helped me to identify some models of data collection as they are used in psychology. Symbols (or constructs) can be understood as socially shared interpretations. They are shared through interpersonal interaction. This interaction requires a mutual orientation of one person to another, so that the acts of one respond to and influence those of the other (Hewitt, 1976). It follows from this approach, then, as well as from the work of Schütz (1967), that an interaction should take place during a psychological enquiry which is concerned with the experience of other people. Before we consider this model, however, I shall deal with some other aspects of the symbolic interactionist approach which merit attention.

People act towards other people according to how they interpret them. People exist for them as a series of experiences they might have with them (Blumer, 1969). People, then, are active interpreters and can reflect on their interpretations. They interact in situations which they themselves define, although the ambiguity of this definition may vary considerably. As they play out their roles, they are not only reactive but creative. They try to understand one another's experience by imagining themselves to be in the other's shoes. Power in such an interaction is essentially a matter of who defines the situation and how. The participants in an interaction may both understand and accept a definition of the situation. However, it is also possible that either or both of them may expend considerable effort in trying to define it according to their own interpretations.

Four models of data collection are suggested by this symbolic interactionist approach. They are illustrated in Figure 1. The Self-Orientation Model can be said to be employed by psychologists when the contributions of both experimenter and subject during an enquiry are determined predominantly by the private interpretations of each participant. This type of interaction, if it can be called that, is determined very little by what takes place between them. In an extreme version of this data collection model, subject and experimenter would be relating to the other only to the extent of waiting until the other stops talking. The Experimenter Orientation Model is employed most often when the experimenters are given a script which they must follow, but the subjects are assumed to be free to respond to the experimenters. Here, the experimenters are governed by their private interpretations, while the subjects are assumed to be responding to the experimenters more often than to their own private interpretations. The Reactive Orientation Model can be applied when both participants in psychological research are reacting to what is currently taking place between them more than to their own private interpretations. Finally, the Mutual Orientation Model is the rarest model of data collection in psychology. It is applied when both the experimenter and the subject contribute something to, and gain something from, the data collection. Their actions are influenced by both their private interpretations and by what takes place between them.

Before examining these models at work, I need to write a few more words about the scope of this book. In the interests of simplicity, I have limited my comments to the collection of data by one person, the experimenter, working with one other person, the subject. Most of what I have to say, however, is relevant for data collectors who work with groups of subjects. Similarly, I have restricted

FIGURE 1

FOUR MODELS OF DATA COLLECTION

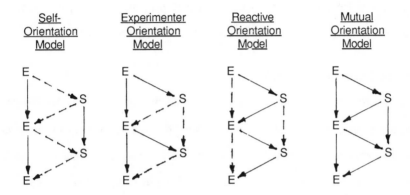

| Self-
Orientation
Model | Experimenter
Orientation
Model | Reactive
Orientation
Model | Mutual
Orientation
Model |

Note: E and S represent the experimenter and the subject of the enquiry interacting over a period of time. The solid lines show the major channels of communication that are open. The broken lines show the communication channels that are, for that model, assumed to be of minor or no importance.

myself to the two well-known figures in psychological research who are known by the titles of "experimenter" and "subject." The experimental method is, after all, the most useful tool for such research. Yet this book is not only for psychologists who work in laboratories. It is also addressed to those who use psychological tests, questionnaires and interviews, and carry out surveys in the field.

The Self-Orientation Model

In this model, relative to the other models, the actions of the experimenter and the subject are rarely contingent on those of the other participant. Each is concerned primarily with himself or herself. Examples are common in many areas of psychology, but especially those involving experimental or interventional studies. Such studies are often carried out with the aim of finding out more about some aspect of the person, such as his or her perception, cognition, or learning; and they have provided us with much worthwhile information. Yet they make some assumptions or interpretations about the people they involve in psychological research, and about their interactions, which must be questioned from a sociophenomenological perspective.

Let us consider one example taken from work on memory. It involves the task of learning lists of common words. Each subject is seated opposite a screen on which slides are projected. The words are exposed on this screen for one second with intervening intervals of about two seconds. A list of words reads something like this: "thief, dentist, stove, skirt, moon, creek (health, vigour), leaf, dish (cottage, vinegar), (hammer, sickle), (soldier, civilian). Commonly associated words have been given in brackets. Comparisons of subjects' responses to these words with those to the words more rarely associated are central to this experiment. The tasks of the experimenter are to give the instructions, show the slides, and record the responses of the subjects.

From the subjects' perspective, the situation is somewhat different. When each list finishes, either a blue or a green slide appears on the screen. They have been told that the blue slide indicates that immediate recall should follow, while the green slide indicates delay. They have been instructed by the experimenter to fill the delay periods by reading aloud six words on a slide to a metronome beat. Under both immediate and delayed recall conditions, the time allowed for the free recall of each list is about one minute. The findings of such a study have bearing on the relative importance of long- and short-term memory (Wickelgren, 1973).

One characteristic of the subject role which is assumed in such a study, and in the Self-Orientation Model generally, is that of passive cooperation. Subjects are expected to respond in any limited way the psychologist has determined for them and not to exceed this restriction. Once they have agreed to participate in the experiment, they make little voluntary contribution to it. The situation has been defined; and it is not to change. Yet, if the situations in which people are observed are so limiting for them, can we validly generalise the results of studies employing this model to other situations, for example, to those of everyday life (Chapanis, 1967)? This form of questioning can also be extended to include the experimenter's role. The experimenter, here, appears to be regarded as passive and as essentially ineffectual. His or her actions during the experiment are limited to some standardised instructions and recording, and the use of some equipment. Often, in Self-Orientation Model studies, this role can now be carried out by computerised data collecting equipment or robots. Perhaps it is a pity that Asimov's (1970) laws of robotics do not apply to human experimenters, especially the law which directs them to promote the welfare of people at all costs!

The experimenters of this model are also assumed to have little or no effect on the results of their enquiries. This interpretation is much disputed, as I shall show in Chapter 4. Meanwhile, let us take another example of a study fitting this model so that these assumptions can be further examined. This example comes from data collection in the field of personality, where personality inventories have been so popular. These techniques require almost no contact between tester and subject. They are also ostensibly subject-centred. Yet they in fact reveal the influence of the interpretations of the psychologists who have designed them. A personality inventory may consist of five hundred or more items such as, "Are you shy with people even at a party?" or "Do people think you are overconscientious about your work?" Each of these questions must be answered, "Yes," "No" or "True," "False" with an occasional "?" being allowed.

Such personality inventories assume that each subject's meaning is the same as that of the psychologist. They also assume that emotionally loaded words such as "shy" and "overconscientious" are not differently interpreted in the differently construed worlds of different subjects. The items or statements are usually selected according to the criterion of meaningfulness for the psychologist, and not for the subjects. Some subjects have tried to point this out. "Many (subjects) said they could write a book on each of the (questionnaire) statements.

When asked to amplify their answers... their response was very scant... often remarks were frankly irrelevant... frequently they consisted of unimportant quibbles over wording" (Eysenck, 1954, pp.125-126). The underlinings are mine; but their meaning is clearly Eysenck's own.

The Self-Orientation Model tends to encourage psychologists to construe both subjects and experimenters inappropriately as passive and ineffectual. Even more importantly, by its title it implies that no interpersonal interaction underlies psychological research and that psychology is not based on relationships between construing people. If little that the experimenter does during the interaction affects the subject, and vice versa, then there can be little relationship between the two to affect the outcome of the study. If this is so, no role expectations can be effective. No power balance can be maintained between the participants since neither exercises any power. Common sense doubts these statements, and empirical evidence (of which some is cited in Chapter 5) questions them. The story of one of Charles Schulz's (1971) cartoons points to this source of invalidation of the Self-Orientation Model.

Linus's older sister Lucy is faced with the problem of devising a science project for the competition at her school in which she intends to win first prize. She selects for study Linus and his security blanket. Her experiment proceeds in this way. She firmly removes the blanket from his grasp, ignoring his anguished outcry. Her instructions to him are: "This is the first test... I'm going to record your reactions." From this point her written record reads as follows: "Ten seconds... indications of fear; thirty seconds... symptoms of panic; forty-two seconds... subject begins to perspire... eyes appear glazed; fifty seconds... subject passes out." She concludes: "Blanket taken from subject... subject loses consciousness due to loss of security." Then she instigates the second, control condition of the experiment, in which she gives Linus back his blanket, and her records read: "Subject recovers."

The Experimenter Orientation Model

While this lampooned experimental interaction demonstrates the Self Orientation Model, another of its striking aspects is its asymmetrical balance of power. Lucy, the experimenter, manipulates the experience of the subject, Linus, and then observes his behaviour. She is in charge of the situation. She is the active organiser and the one who determines what will happen. Linus is the powerless victim of her efforts and cannot even question them. Such a data collection is best represented by the second model described here, the Experimenter Orientation Model. This model assumes the experimenter to be an active construer and to be acting upon the subjects. The subjects' actions and experiences in such a study are thought to be primarily a function of what the experimenter has done to them. Their own history and goals, and therefore their construed meanings, are considered to be relatively unimportant.

A study of person perception which is often included in introductory psychology courses will serve as an example. From the students' perspective, the data are collected like this. As one of their classes is about to start, a staff member (the experimenter) announces that the usual tutor or instructor is away and that the class will be taken by a new tutor. The tutor is introduced as a graduate student, twenty-six years old and married. He is said to have had a few years of teaching experience. The experiment continues: "People who know him consider him to be a rather <u>cold</u> person, industrious, critical, practical and determined. This introduction is almost the same each time the tutor is introduced to different classes; the only difference is that sometimes he is described as <u>warm</u> rather than cold, the aim being to examine the effect of these two contrasting and experimentally created first impressions.

The new tutor then leads a discussion in each class during which the experimenter records the amount of interaction with him. Finally, after the new tutor leaves, the experimenter asks the subjects for their impressions of him. They fill out rating scales, the items of which are chosen because they are meaningful to the psychologist but not to the subjects. The "cold" tutor is generally associated by the subjects with words like self-centred, unsociable, humourless, and irritable. They interact less with him than when he was described as "warm." Initial expectations can be very powerful, and so, it seems, can experimenters.

The relationship between experimenter and subjects in this Model consists not of an interaction, but a one-way action. The experimenter influences; the subjects are influenced. In this example, the experimenter is particularly powerful because he or she is also a staff member and the subjects are students in his or her course. This is a common situation in psychology (Smart, 1966). In it subjects are not really free to leave the experiment if they wish to do so. They are again assumed to be passively cooperative and to accept the interpretations of others without question. Finally, they are not regarded fully as construing people since their capacities to reflect on their own interpretations of events during the research are ignored. The role of the experimenter is more extensive in the Experimenter Orientation Model since he or she is called upon not only to give instructions and record, but to influence the subjects. Yet the range of choice of the experimenter is still considerably limited.

This person perception study which I have described does at least accept some part of the interaction between subject and experimenter, since it makes direct use of it in investigating the influence of the experimenter on the subjects. Other studies tend to distort it. An example from physiological psychology demonstrates this. The aim of a study like this would be to relate the occurrence of certain physiological events to the occurrence of certain behavioural events, for example, changes in cortical evoked potential and changes in vigilance. In such a study, each subject enters a room with much equipment in it, the machinery for the presentation of the vigilance task and for recording, coding and analysing electroencephalogram (EEG) signals. The experimenter cleans several areas of the subjects' scalps with alcohol, pushing their hair out of the way in order to do so. He fixes the electrodes on the scalp, fills them with electrode jelly for good conductivity, and connects them to the amplifier and recorder. At least, that is what the experimenter construes himself as doing. What the subjects construe him as doing is a question unanswered in the reports of such studies. Nor are the characteristics of the relationship which must be all this while developing between experimenter and subject recorded.

To return to the construed world of the subjects, the vigilance task they undertake while prepared in this way takes up to an hour and a half. They are required to watch flashes on a screen and press a key when they see dim flashes as distinct from bright ones. The experimenter sounds a tone from time to time. It is a boring task. It must be, in order to test their vigilance. The subjects

have little contact with the experimenter during this period, apart from hearing his

auditory signals. Usually, the findings from such an experiment are that declines

in the accuracy of subjects on this task are associated with increased frequency

and decreased amplitude in their EEG waves. The auditory stimulation affects

the nature of the association. In other words, relationships between observed

behaviour and observed physiological events are demonstrated. This study, like

all the others cited in this chapter, provides data fascinating to research

psychologists and of considerable value to those who apply psychology as well.

This study, just one example of the Experimenter Orientation Model, is

based on the assumption or interpretation that any communication between

experimenter and subject is in one direction only. Yet there is an interaction

between the two which has been called a hidden dialogue, since it is not

necessarily openly verbalised (Lyons, 1970). It is true that in this model the chief

message comes from the experimenter who says, in effect, to the subjects: "If you

do what I tell you and produce the right results, I'll be pleased with you." Yet the

subjects respond in many ways, according to their interpretations of the situation.

They may think: "OK, let's get this over with," or "You're sure I can't get a shock

from all this?" or "Why the hell should I?" Whichever hidden dialogue is started, it

may be as confounding to the overt aims of the research as is the hidden agenda

of a committee meeting to its overt aims.

The Reactive Orientation Model

If such interaction is ignored, as it is in studies using the Self-Orientation

Model of data collection, then there must be a model which allows for it. In fact, there are two, both of which remain to be dealt with. The Reactive Orientation Model, to be considered now, construes the interaction between experimenter and subject to be the prime influence on any resulting data. It is considered to be more important than the personal interpretations of either of the two participants. Data collected within this model rely little on any reflection by either experimenter or subject about what is happening. They are supposed simply to react, chiefly to each other. A single example makes this clear. This example again comes from the area of learning.

One of the most used learning paradigms is Skinner's operant conditioning paradigm. It has been employed even to change attitudes, although it is only one of many approaches to attitude change (Insko, 1967). This design is often used with students as subjects, but also with students as experimenters. Let us take the experimenter's point of view this time. The experimenter interviews each student subject about some issue relevant to students. She presents a series of prepared statements about this issue and asks her subjects to agree or disagree with each of them. Usually half of the statements favour one argument and the other half, the opposing argument. The experimenter rewards the subjects by saying "Good!" when they respond as if supporting one of the arguments. In order to control for the effects of different types of arguments, the study is often run so as to reinforce some of the students for supporting one argument. Then the others are reinforced for supporting the other argument. The patterns of responses of the subjects are usually successfully altered so as to demonstrate the effects of the verbal reinforcement, regardless of their original attitudes. It is not known if their constructs or interpretations change, but their behaviour does.

In this study it is as if subject and experimenter respond only according to each other's responses and not according to their construing of their current situation, their already existing constructs or their goals. But can this be? There is, for one thing, an interplay of role expectations between experimenter and subject which is very much part of their current experience in any psychological research. Subjects are expected, by both the experimenters and the subjects themselves, to be biddable, to conform to the ordinary rules of politeness and to refrain from asking any questions about the study. In return, both subjects and experimenters expect experimenters to "run" the experiment confidently and smoothly, without responding as if to another construing person or as if they were themselves construing people. Where these role expectations come from it is hard to say. Yet if Schulz can expect to raise a laugh with his story about Lucy and Linus, it would seem that they are very commonly associated with psychological research.

In the Reactive Orientation Model, subject and experimenter are also construed as not having personal memories which affect their experimental interaction (Connell, 1977). Yet Linus's frightening memories of Lucy were an integral part of her study. In the unlikely event that bumbling but kind Charlie Brown had conducted the experiment, the memories Linus had of him might have made it less catastrophic. And what of the goals of experimenters? What of their expectations? Lucy expected Linus to faint, and faint he did. To conduct the study of attitude change described, I would rather select experimenters who believe in the power of reinforcement than those who do not. Yet my findings might not be valid.

When this Reactive Orientation Model of data collection is employed, it does appear somewhat ridiculous that experimenters try to obtain from subjects their informed consent to experiments. We have all seen published accounts of such studies, which read like this: "Informed consent was obtained from the subjects, and they were aware that they could withdraw from the experiment at any time." How can subjects be asked to give informed consent if they are denied the capacity to construe the events related to data collection? How can experimenters "know" that the subjects are "informed" if they lack that same capacity?

The Mutual Orientation Model

The Mutual Orientation Model of data collection is, I believe, potentially the most appropriate model for a psychology about people who make interpretations and reflect on those interpretations. It permits the use of "informed consent" because it allows for the personal interpretation of both experimenter and subject. It also takes into account their interaction, as other models have not done. It assumes that the acts of both experimenter and subject respond to and influence one another. They are influenced both by their personal interpretations and by what takes place between them. It is hard to find an example of the use of such a model. Data collection based on Piaget's (1930) approach to intelligence seems the most appropriate example.

Piaget has maintained that at a certain stage in the normal development of children, they come to realise that the physical attributes of an object may remain the same although the form of that object changes. It is not until children have grasped this principle of conservation that they can use more complex cognitive processes. Let us consider the conservation of weight. The six- or seven-year-old children being tested for this would experience the research in the following way. They are greeted by an adult experimenter who works individually with them. They are introduced to a balancing scale and given opportunities to observe for themselves what happens when things are weighed. They are then given two balls of differently coloured plasticene and shown that, since they balance each other exactly, they weigh the same. Then the experimenter reshapes one of the plasticene balls, saying: "Now I change the ball into a cup. Do you think the ball weighs more? Do you think they weigh the same? Or do you think that one (pointing to the reshaped plasticene) weighs more?" The children give their answers and are asked, "Why do you think so?" The interaction continues until the experimenter has answers which she considers herself to understand.

If children report that the changed object weighs the same as the unchanged object, they have demonstrated that they have attained conservation of weight. They may have given a perceptual cue as their reason, by referring to some directly observable feature of the objects. Or they may have achieved a symbolic solution by relating this event to previous events. At a more complex level yet, they may have provided a symbolic/logical answer, by referring to a stated principle. The principle in this case would be that nothing has been added or taken away. It is the experimenter's task to classify the children's reactions into one of these three categories. But first she must ensure that the children are adequately expressing their concepts within the interaction. The experimenter must also ensure that it is the children's concepts and not her own which are analysed.

In such a study the subjects are also regarded as active choosers and creators of meaning. They know and know that they know. This is so even though its aims are similar to the aims of other research which has used rather different and more limiting models of data collection. Psychologists following Piaget are concerned with how people think, just like the psychologists who use the memory paradigm described earlier. Yet this does not prevent them from accepting that subjects are construing people who can actively contribute to their research. This Mutual Orientation Model of data collection also allows acceptance of experimenters as construing people, as can be seen in the example described.

The capacities of experimenters to know and reflect on their knowledge are also given full play. They are required to listen to the reasoning of the child subjects, to probe quietly without asking leading questions, and to clarify what meaning the subjects themselves are placing on their experiences. This is a highly skilled experimenter role. Experimenters are required to determine whether their subjects have made clear to them their present line of reasoning and to use their own judgement in determining into what category their responses fall. The experimenters' capacities for interpretation and reflection are brought into play in this model of data collection as they are by few others.

All of this takes place through the interaction of subject and experimenter. This interaction is unique amongst those we have examined for a reason that it may at first seem flippant to mention. Both subject and experimenter are free to express doubts and make mistakes. We have seen how in other models experimenters must be confident and subjects cannot ask questions. This is not so for this model, in which, for example, the experimenters in the enquiry outlined can admit to the children that they do not understand them. The children similarly can make up their own responses since there are no "right" answers. Even the questions of subjects are valued since they indicate some of their current thinking. The Mutual Orientation Model does away with some of the unnecessarily rigid forms of interaction in psychological research and frees both of the participants for a more creative interplay.

The Models and Their Assumptions

In Chapter 1, I maintained that our current models of data collection tend to determine the subject matter of our studies, rather than that subject matter determining our choice of methods. In this chapter, support has been found for that position from my analysis of the data collection models now in use. Four such models have been described in terms of the assumptions or anticipatory interpretations inherent in them. They are, in essence, models of communication. In the Self-Orientation Model, only the channels of communication within each experimenter and subject are open. In the Experimenter Orientation Model, only those controlled by the experimenter are open. In the Reactive Orientation Model, the communication channels between subject and experimenter are open but those within each are closed. It is only in the Mutual Orientation Model that both private reflections on interpretations and exchanges of interpretations between the two participants are possible.

Table 1 presents an evaluation of the status of these four models in relation to some of the assumptions revealed as questionable by personal construct psychology and other sociophenomenological approaches. They are divided into those relating to subjects, experimenters, and their interactions. The Self-Orientation Model appears to invoke the somewhat dubious assumption that subjects are passively cooperative and accept the interpretations of others in preferences to their own. It also makes similar assumptions about experimenters. Neither of our principal figures is viewed as an active construer. Nor are any of the interpersonal implications of their interaction fully accepted. Communication is not apparently taking place through socially shared interpretations. The Experimenter Orientation Model, on the other hand, appears to give greater scope to experimenters as active construers and as reflective knowers. The subjects of this model, however, are permitted none of these capacities. Also, most of the assumptions about the experimental interaction are debatable. This is a model which fully exploits an imbalance of power in favour of experimenters, who appear, at least, to define the experimental situation.

The Reactive Orientation Model gives full recognition to the nature of that interaction. Yet studies employing it tend to involve questionable assumptions about subjects and experimenters. Specifically, this model assumes that the capacities of both subjects and experimenters to construe and to reflect on their resulting constructs are unimportant and tends to ignore them. The symbolic interactionists would dispute this. Of the ten questionable assumptions listed in Table 1, all are accepted by at least some of the first three models. None of these models, therefore, is free from distorting assumptions. The only model of data collection which appears to be free from them is the Mutual Orientation Model.

TABLE 1

QUESTIONABLE ASSUMPTIONS INHERENT IN THE
DATA COLLECTION MODELS

Sources of Questionable Assumptions	Self-Orientation Model	Experimenter Orientation Model	Reactive Orientation Model	Mutual Orientation Model
Subjects				
are passively cooperative	x	x		
accept other's interpretations	x	x		
capacity for reflection is unimportant		x	x	
Experimenters				
may appear active but are ineffectual	x			
accept other's interpretations	x			
capacity for reflection is unimportant			x	
Subject/Experimenter Interaction				
is not inter-personal	x	x		
does not affect the data	x	x		
involves no role expectations	x	x		
has no weighted balance of power	x			

Many psychologists would argue that the other models have served us well so far, and they have. But we are searching for models of data collection suited to ourselves and our subject matter (Kuhn, 1962). We are seeking to interprete the interpreters. Those models which reduce that subject matter to less than actively construing people do not suit it well. Models which assume subjects to be less than human and prohibit experimenters from fulfilling their potential as human beings are in danger of producing a psychology of less than the person. Further, when the relationship between subject and experimenter is not allowed to be fully interactive, then it can bear little resemblance to what people find out about other people when they relate freely to them. Unquestioning acceptance of these anticipatory interpretations is unlikely to result in a generally relevant psychology which is acknowledged as being by and about construing people.

References

Asimov, I. (1970). I, Robot. Greenwich, Connecticut: Fawcett Crest.

Blumer, H. (1969). Symbolic interactionism: Perspective and method. Englewood Cliffs, New Jersey: Prentice-Hall.

Chapanis, A. (1967). The relevance of laboratory studies to practical situations. Ergonomics, 10, 537-577.

Connell, R.W. (1977). All were ignorant of the aim of the experiment: A modest excursion in the sociology of a psychology. Australian Psychological Society Division of Clinical Psychologists Bulletin, 9, 13-17.

Eysenck, H.J. (1954). The psychology of politics. London: Routledge & Kegan Paul.

Hewitt, J.P. (1976). Self and society: A symbolic interactionist social psychology. Boston: Allyn & Bacon.

Insko, C.A. (1967). Theories of attitude change. New York: Appleton-Century-Crofts.

Kuhn, T. (1962). The structure of scientific revolutions. Chicago: University of Chicago Press.

Lyons, J. (1970). The hidden dialogue in experimental research. Journal of Phenomenological Psychology, 1, 19-29.

Mead, G.H. (1962). Mind, self and society. Chicago: University of Chicago Press.

Piaget, J. (1930). The child's conception of physical causality. New York: Harcourt Brace & Co.

Schulz, C.M. (1971). You're the greatest, Charlie Brown. Greenwich, Conn.: Fawcett.

Schütz, A. (1967). The phenomenology of the social world. Chicago: Northwestern University Press.

Smart, R. (1966). Subject selection bias in psychological research. Canadian Psychologist, 7a, 115-121.

Wickelgren, W.A. (1973). The long and short of memory. Psychological Bulletin, 80, 425-438.

CHAPTER 3

SUBJECTS AS CONSTRUING PEOPLE

Do we make the same assumptions about the subjects in psychological enquiries

as we make about ourselves?

Do we define the stimuli for the subjects or do they?

Why do subjects participate in our enquiries?

Can we have confidence in the reports of our subjects?

Are we making the best use of our subjects?

That psychologists, as scientists, make interpretations of their work and its subject matter is now established. That the subject of psychological experiments often appears to bear the connotations of "one who is subjected" is not an interpretation, however, to be accepted in the same sense. Its implicit assumptions must be considered carefully, because of its implications for psychology. This chapter, in fact, makes an opposing assumption and examines its implications. My assumption is that the subject is an actively construing person.

The reflexivity of this interpretation of experimenters and subjects is first noted. Then the effects of it on psychologists' views of their subject will be examined, yielding images of the subject as an active chooser, a maker of interpretations, and a reflective knower. I shall also refer to the empirical evidence for these effects. These findings will be viewed from two perspectives. The traditional psychological and the personal construct psychology perspectives each provide some recommendations involving methods which psychologists may choose to use.

As the Experimenter, so the Subject

In Wundt's original experiments the role of the subject was considered to be more important than that of the experimenter (Danziger, 1985). Since then, however, psychologists have become uneasy about our ways of viewing our subjects. At the beginning of this century their role as "stupid automatons" was noted (Pierce, 1908). A quarter of a century later it was remarked that, unlike chemical substances which are apparently more amenable to the will of the experimenter, the human subjects of psychology "have minds of their own"

(Rosenweig, 1933). This characteristic appears to have been regarded as a misfortune by some psychologists, although our attention has been drawn to the opportunities such capacities offer (Adair, 1973). This view is as common in psychological studies of children as it is of adults (Salmon, 1979).

The tendency to consider researcher and experimenter, on the one hand, and subject, on the other, as completely different beings may have been the result of some misleading notion of objectivity (Landfield, 1970). But for psychologists who must have considered themselves to be construers and reflectors to have denied these capacities to their subjects is strange indeed! It is only with Kelly's (1955) statement of the concept of reflexivity that a direct challenge to the position has been made. Psychologists are now required to work within a perspective which applies as much to themselves as to others. It is only fair to point out that some early psychologists, like Freud and Tolman, did achieve reflexivity. That Tolman's concept of cognitive maps could be applied equally as well to himself as to his subjects is at least as remarkable as Freud's insightful application of the same methodology to himself that he used with his patients. Tolman's subjects were often laboratory rats, not human patients in a consulting room. As he tried to predict their behaviour, Tolman actually employed an approach which we might now call empathic: "If I were a rat . . ." (Tolman, 1938).

Having alluded to psychoanalysis and one of the classical learning theories, it now seems appropriate for me to turn to the third force psychology (Buhler, 1965). How does humanism relate to the phenomenological perspective? Of course it is much closer to it in many respects than it is, for example, to the behaviourist tradition with which it is often compared (Hitt, 1969). How close, it is difficult to determine. There is an imprecision and lack of systematisation in humanistic theories of the person, involved as they are with goals of personal growth. Psychologists like Rogers, while part of the third force, may not be truly phenomenologists (Kuenzli, 1959; Fischer, 1976). The histories of humanism and phenomenology have been contrasted (Misiak & Sexton, 1973). It seems that humanism has been espoused by psychologists as a way of redressing the balance between the sciences and the humanities (Cardno, 1966). The humanistic approach involves a positive view of the subject as a person (Cantril, 1967) which is, to some extent, in accord with the assumptions which I am proposing in this book. But in its determinedly positive attitude (Buhler & Allen, 1972), it is far from the search for viable alternative views of the individual which is carried out by personal construct psychologists.

Despite this crucial difference, humanism and personal construct psychology have many points of agreement. One important construct acceptable to both has been stated as follows. "We learn more about man by assuming him to be an active agent than by assuming him to be a passive victim of circumstances" (Child, 1973, p.68). Child cites an interesting comparison between workers in the field of hypnosis who adopted one or the other of these assumptions. In the latter camp were Hull and his co-workers, who produced a habit theory of hypnosis (Hull, 1933). This theory accounted for what appeared to be the learned nature of trance behaviour, but it added little to what was known about the nature of hypnosis. In contrast, the work of the Hilgards (1965; 1970) was able to go much further because of their acceptance of the view that people's descriptions of their experiences and their reflections on them could be useful to scientific study. Their resulting picture of hypnosis, which was richer than the habit-based picture, involved descriptions of alterations in experience. People, then, were construed by the Hilgards as active experiencers. Rogers has said of his relationship with a client: "In so far as I see him as an object, (he) will tend to become only an object" (Rogers, 1961). This has sometimes been the fate of the subject of psychological research.

Active Choosers

This objectifying of the subjects, or dehumanising of people, has enabled psychologists to perceive them as nonactive. Just how absurd the end-product could become has been made clear in this poem, reminiscent of W.H. Auden, addressed to the Unknown Subject.

> "He was found by researchers to be
> a perfect model of passivity,
> and all research on him concludes
> he was cooperative and didn't intrude,
> didn't ask questions or try to divine
> the hidden intent of the experimental design . . . "

(Richards, 1972, p.22)

(I could not bring myself to disrupt its rhythm by dealing with the sexist language of the poem.) The contrast of the view expressed here with the personal construct perspective on the subject is sharp. The latter focusses on a person with a construed world combining past experience and future goals with hypotheses about the present.

Yet even the stimuli to which the subject is intended to respond are often defined from the point of view of the experimenter and not that of the subject

(Perrot, 1977). Some attempts have been made to capture the subject's view. They include work on how stressful subjects perceive various experimental procedures to be (Farr & Seaver, 1975). The majority of a sample of subjects of social psychological research were found to have preferred not to have been involved (Wilson & Downerstein, 1976). Comparison of subjects' with experimenters' views on certain ethical issues in human research have also been carried out (Sullivan & Deiker, 1973). Far too few of these studies of the experience of psychological research are, however, presently available.

Subjects come to the psychological enquiry with a variety of their own "in order to" and "because" motives. This is especially so if they have volunteered (Rosenthal & Rosnow, 1969). They may have agreed to participate in order to avoid more disturbing alternatives, to ingratiate themselves with the experimenter, or for the pay (Criswell, 1958). Or they may have decided to do so because they were bored. They may even have had little choice about participating and, like many psychology student subjects, be fulfilling a course requirement. As well as the attainment of rewards due, subjects may be concerned about presenting themselves in a favourable light and about discovering what the experimenter is up to and what the experiment is about. Psychologists tend to view subjects as automated data production units. In fact, my rat-running friends and colleagues are envious of the ability of my human subjects to feed and water themselves. Yet there is "a set of inferential and interpretive activities on the part of the subject to penetrate the experimenter's inscrutability" (Riecken, 1962, p.31).

Subjects who are active construers can affect the behaviour of the experimenter. "Accomplice subjects" have been found to influence their experimenters (Rosenthal, 1967). Questionnaire responders have also reacted to and influenced conductors of surveys when they have chosen to be yea-sayers or nay-sayers or to respond in a socially desirable rather than an honestly self-reporting way (Edwards, 1957; Bloch, 1965). Four subject roles may be chosen by subjects in an experiment (Weber & Cook, 1972). These are the role of the good subject, or the confirmer of experimental hypotheses; the bad subject, or disconfirmer of those hypotheses; the faithful subject, of which the passive type is very docile and the active is very honest; and the apprehensive subject. There is considerable evidence for the last role being played often by subjects; we will look more closely at its effects below. Little evidence of the existence of the faithful subject was said to be available and none at all for the good and bad subject roles.

There is, however, some evidence that subjects choose to cooperate or not to cooperate with their experimenter. The behaviour of subjects who were helping in a rat-running experiment was observed (Penner et al., 1973). They chose to respond much more obediently to experimenters whom they perceived to be competent than to those they perceived to be incompetent. (Believing a "nervous" rat to have died in the course of the experiment was thought to have decreased their confidence in the experimenter). Further, subjects have been found to cooperate with experimenters to the extent of behaving so as to confirm their hypotheses (Sigall, Aronsen & Van Hoose, 1970). Such cooperation occurred only when the subject's own goals were better met by cooperating and not when they were not. A subject makes such choices within the context of his or her construed world.

Interpreters

Each subject may be viewed as a maker of meaning, an organiser of his or her experiences of events (Salmon, 1980). In terms of personal construct psychology, each person works at actively elaborating his or her interpretations of the world. Indeed, that is the personal construct definition of aggressive behaviour. It consists of those actions which serve to provide more alternatives between which the person can choose. There is another definition by personal construct psychology of an emotion which is of interest to us here, too, that is, anxiety. If events occur which cannot be understood by a person's construct system, then anxiety occurs (Kelly, 1955). A subject who cannot interpret effectively the events he or she experiences is therefore likely to be a distressed subject. We can only guess at the guilt-related anxiety generated in the subjects who played the "warders" in the famous prison study (Zimbardo, 1973). The central constructs they applied to themselves were probably not able to encompass their experience of their own hostile and punitive behaviour in the warder role (Savin, 1973).

It seems that most subjects in psychological experiments have hypotheses about what is happening to them and why (Mair, 1970). This is so even when the data are collected using the Self-Orientation or Experimenter Orientation Models. If you find this proposition difficult to accept, try volunteering for the subject role yourself. I have participated in a series of experiments designed to ascertain the significance of supraspinal activity in reflexes. The reflex under study has been that of the Achilles tendon. As my body responded to the tap of the hammer I found myself hypothesising about the latency and magnitude of my kick. Should it, for example, be bigger or smaller, faster or slower, when the warning buzzer and light are presented simultaneously or at different times? And what about the order in which those different patterns of stimuli were presented to me? How was that arrived at by the experimenters? That it was randomly generated did not occur to me for quite a few minutes! Now these are the experiences of a psychologist as a subject and not of a naive subject. Yet they serve to show how, as a subject, I found myself constantly and actively endeavouring to make sense of my experience. From the viewpoint of the symbolic interactionists, I was acting towards the objects of my experience according to the interpretations I placed on them. When I could not construe them effectively I struggled to create more useful interpretations of my situation.

Subjects are not often asked about their expectations (Epstein, Suedfield & Silverstein, 1973). It is important that this gap in psychological research be filled because, as the personal construct psychologists have taught us ﹍ understand the behaviour of a person we need to know how he or she interprets it. At the more concrete level, empirical demonstrations of the effects of subjects' expectations on their experimental acts -- like those of the effects of psychiatric patients' expectations on the course of subsequent treatment (Frank, 1973) -- have been made. For example, subjects have compared a standard tone to each of nine randomly presented tones which differed from it (Zoble & Lehman, 1969). Differing expectations about which stimulus tones would match the standard tone were given to the subjects. As hypothesised, they did influence their matching.

The personality "traits" of subjects, those relatively stable ways of viewing the world which they bring to the experiment, help to determine the interpretations they make. These "traits" may consist of the intrapsychic defense mechanisms the patient is said to display during a clinical assessment by a psychologist (Schafer, 1954). Because the psychologist is testing hypotheses the assessment may be thought of as a series of experiments. Alternatively, the "traits" may be more socially oriented traits, such as authoritarianism (Marquis, 1973) or dogmatism (Lazlo & Rosenthal, 1971). In the study of the latter "trait," the task for the subject was Rosenthal's standard photograph rating task, and experimenters were led to expect positive or negative ratings. Subjects with high dogmatism scores were found to be more susceptible than low scorers to the experimenter expectancy effect (of which more will follow in Chapter 4).

Subjects interpret their experiences in many ways. For example, they may examine their own previous related experiences or try to account for the behaviour of the other people involved. Attribution theorists have pointed out that people do not simply observe, but infer or attribute aspects of the experience of others also (Jones & Davis, 1965). This inference occurs through matching of the observed behaviour with constructs from the subject's own earlier experience (De Charms, 1968). Subjects also examine the characteristics of the total situation in which they find themselves. Orne (1962), whom we have seen to perceive the subject as a construer and interpreter, has labelled these cueing characteristics, demand characteristics. They may include factors as varied as the setting of the experiment and rumours about it. They may also include information implicit in the way it is run, for example, the experimenter's presence or absence (Musante & Anker, 1972). It is impossible to eliminate these demand characteristics from psychological research. Subjects can never be neutral towards an experiment because they construe it in its total context of their experience of past and present events.

Reflective Knowers

Some of the effects of subjects being able to reflect on their own experience are discussed here, especially their suspiciousness, their need to maintain self-esteem and their evaluation apprehension. The subject observes the transaction between the experimenter and himself or herself and tries to construe it so as to make sense of it. When this is not readily done, the subject may become aggressive, self-derogatory or just plain anxious.

There is evidence that subjects become suspicious when taking part in a psychological experiment (Schultz, 1969), although this hypothesis has not always been confirmed (John, 1984). If subjects themselves act according to plans, as Schütz would have us believe, they are likely to ascribe plans to an experimenter: "What is he planning for me?" This suspicious reaction may be because of some aspect of the experimenter, for example, perceived disinterestedness on his or her part. It may also be due to the message style, or the content of the instructions, or some characteristic of the experimental setting (McGuire, 1969). Suspiciousness also arises in construing subjects when deception is practiced by the researcher (Stricker, Messick & Jackson, 1969). The effects of subject suspiciousness are difficult to pinpoint. It seems very likely to elicit defensive experiencing and acting from them. It may lead to the demand characteristics, or the situation, or their own opinions becoming more salient. It may also lead to a misleading set of expectations being established, or at the very least to some distraction of their attention from the experimental task. Whichever of these occurs, the effect of subjects' suspiciousness is likely to be that they neither interpret nor, consequently, respond to the research procedure in the way in which the psychologist intended.

The next two consequences of subjects being knowers to be discussed are intimately related since they concern their attitudes to themselves, to that aspect of their construed world with which they most identify. People need to feel good about themselves (Rogers, 1959). Subjects, then, given a choice, are likely to refuse to participate in experiments which lower their self-esteem. This need for self-esteem is associated with a need for positive regard from others, a need to be accepted by others. It is no wonder that evaluation apprehension has been found in subjects (Rosenberg, 1965).

It has been argued that subjects often approach experiments with the expectation that the experimenter may be evaluating their emotional adequacy or their personal adjustment. I am inclined, however, to think that their expectations do not always have to hold these precise sources of fear for evaluation apprehension to occur. Whatever the content of the expectations, subjects can become primarily concerned that they gain a positive evaluation from the experimenter, or, at the very least, not a negative one.

Such a concern can, of course, produce a systematic bias in almost any collection of psychological data (Rosenberg, 1969). This is especially so if the required behaviour is indicated by the experimenter (Rosenthal, 1976). When one researcher interacted with and listened to his subjects after his experiments, he found he was often asked questions like: "How did I go?" (Rosenberg, 1965).

65

He also found that they were often preoccupied with questions like: "What was the real purpose of the experiment?" Subjects do try to construe their world meaningfully.

As a researcher, I have recently been using a method in which I ask subjects to discuss freely events of common interest to us. The instructions are open-ended: "I want you to talk about what your life is like at the moment." If a subject finds it hard to talk, I add a construct which I believe every subject uses in some way: "Tell me about the good things and the bad." This adds as little as possible of the experimenter's or researcher's constructs to the report. This contamination is further controlled in the content analysis which the experimenter then applies to the report (Viney, 1981; Viney & Westbrook, 1981). This method of data collection has proved effective in tapping subjects' interpretations of a range of life changes (Viney, 1980), their reactions to the crises of illness (Viney, 1983a, 1985) and unemployment (Viney, 1983b), as well as assessing their psychosocial maturity (Viney & Tych, 1985). Not all the effects of the status of subjects as reflective knowers lead to problems like those which have been noted. As can be seen from my own research, it is this very capacity which makes the reflecting subject our primary source of data. It makes introspection and subsequent self-report possible.

Some Traditional Psychological Perspectives

Before dealing with the findings reported in this chapter, I would like to continue briefly with the topic of introspection, this time viewing it from a traditional psychological perspective -- for it has been advocated as a useful method from within that tradition (Stout, 1938; Burt, 1962). A history of introspection has already been prepared (Boring, 1953); there is no need for another here. I would remind you only of its use by psychologists like Titchener, and of Freud's self-analysis. There are, however, problems in its use, and they should be made clear.

One of these involves the assumption that there is a private, construed world of experience of the subject to be tapped by introspection. This is fundamental to personal construct psychologists. And, if there is such a construed world, can it effectively be made public by introspection? Many more traditional psychologists would answer this question negatively. In self-report, subjects may be fallible, may be influenced by repression or rationalisation, or may give culturally determined responses which are somewhat ethnocentric (Bakan, 1967). If these characteristics of subjects are indeed inherent in them, we shall have to find ways of dealing with them in our methods.

The purpose to which introspection is put must also be an important consideration. It may be used directly in research, as Titchener attempted. It may also be used as experience to illuminate the observed behaviour of others, as Tolman used it. Finally, it may be effective as a source of new hypotheses about both behaviour and experience. I suspect that many psychologists use it in this way. Introspection is still employed as an adjunct in traditional laboratory-based experiments and will probably be with us for a long time to come. It is, in fact, one practice in which traditional psychologists accept the assumption of subjects being active, interpreting people and do not underrate their capacity to reflect on their experience.

That is why I began this section with the topic of introspection; it provides an example of the reflective capacities of subjects being valued by psychologists. In order to test hypotheses, psychologists try to conceive and run experiments in which the effects of all relevant variables which are not under investigation by them are controlled. The result of this is sometimes control of the subjects, too, so that they cannot behave like a person because their experience is not currently that of a person. Psychology is in danger of being the only science to produce a view of its subject matter which is more limited than the prevailing commonsense view (Bannister, 1966).

Two other distorting effects of the assumption that the subject can be treated as a non-person are also important. The first is that when the subject is construed as an object "to be poked, prodded, manipulated and measured" (Schultz, 1969, p.217), the relationship between the two participants in the psychological experiment becomes that of person to thing. The implications of this for psychology will be explored in Chapter 5. The second effect relates to the influence that psychologists may have on how people construe other people. There is no doubt that Freud's view of people has been exceedingly influential in modern Western society. By the same token, women and men of the future may come to construe themselves as the subjects of today's psychological experiments. "Keep telling a man he is nothing but an oversized rat, and he will start growing whiskers and bite your finger" (Köstler, 1969, p.5).

Now I shall return, more specifically, to the subject's personal attributes as they are beginning to emerge in this chapter. It is interesting to note the attempts of traditional psychologists to deal with them as "subject error," as if they were not the very heart of psychology (Baloff & Becker, 1967). Many authors contributed to

Rosenthal and Rosnow's (1969) book, of which the title is important: Artifact in Behavioural Research. They appear to view these tendencies of subjects to construe situations in certain ways as extraneous conditions which should be eliminated from every experiment. If they cannot be, as I maintain, then their effects, traditional psychology has it, should be carefully controlled. It has been claimed that most of these "artifacts" occur because subjects are aware that they are participating in psychological research (Campbell, 1969). Attention has therefore been given to devising disguised or deceptive techniques to circumvent this awareness.

There are three points that I would make in regard to this traditional approach. The first concerns the suggestion of deception. Surely field research provides a much more viable and ethically acceptable method of avoiding the subjects' construed world of "self in experiment" (Bickman & Henchy, 1972). Second, I would inquire of them why they want to partial out the effects of such characteristics, when multivariate techniques of statistical analysis make it possible for them to be incorporated into any experimental design (Overall & Klett, 1972; Boch, 1975). I make this suggestion, not because controlling one source of subject bias often introduces another (Lester, 1969), but because of my assumption that the subject is an active construer. The expectations of subjects can be assessed, just as expectations of patients entering psychiatric treatment have been (Freeman & Viney, 1977). If these "subject errors" are an integral part of the person, the subject of psychology, then it is important that we know what their effects on any dependent variable of interest are, alone and in interaction with other independent variables.

My third point refers to the types of controls which have traditionally been practised. They have tended to be of an all-or-none variety, denying subjects their interpretive role. Orne, however, faithful to his assumption that the subject is actively engaged in making sense of his or her experience, studies these "subject errors" in their own right. While he does so, he enlists the aid of the subject as a construer and communicator. He has developed his three types of quasi controls for the effects of demand characteristics (Orne, 1969). One involves a post-experimental enquiry in which he elicits the cooperation of subjects and taps into other interpretations. In another, the subjects are asked to respond as if they have had the experimental treatment. In the other quasi control, Orne also makes use of the subjects' capacities to reflect on their own experience by asking them to simulate the experiment with experimenters blind to its purpose and hypotheses. Active, cooperating subjects, then, can be very helpful to psychologists (Mair, 1977; Mischel, 1977).

The Personal Construct Perspective

This enlisting of the cooperation of the subjects to share their unique experience with the experimenter was probably fostered by social psychologists (Argyris, 1968) as well as by personal construct psychologists. Yet, it is a trend which is now apparent in general psychology as well. Most subjects are likely to be happy to engage in any opportunity to extend their construct systems. It may well be that the most powerful motive prompting them to engage in psychological research is their curiosity about what will happen and about how they will deal with it when it does. For this reason, let us examine next some research which has made use of the ability of subjects to cooperate.

Let us take, for example, the development of the Joy Scale (Meadow, 1975). It is one of the standard, item-screened, factor-analysed questionnaires common in the area of personality and individual differences. Yet the items it contains were drawn up, not by a psychologist, but on the basis of dimensions of joy encountered by subjects as they construed their world. Another example has been provided in the area of social psychology. The concern was with subjects' experience of small group interaction, not with the perceptions of some objective observer (Rinn, 1966). After each group session the members filled out blanks with sentence stems involving "The group...," "The leader...," "One member...," and "I..." When the series of encounter sessions was over, these sentences were given to the group members, who sorted through them to establish dimensions of group interaction and then individually rated their own interactions. The resulting scales were amenable to most forms of statistical analysis, yet their content remained true to the interpretations of the group members.

Another solution to this problem of how to make meaningful comparisons between different, idiosyncratic accounts of experience without destroying their uniqueness is Kelly's Role Construct Repertory Technique. As originally developed, it was a simple technique based on the bipolar nature of constructs (Kelly, 1955). He asked his subjects to think of people who filled important roles in their lives which he specified (for example, mother, father, husband, wife, boss, friend, disliked person). He then asked for a comparison of three of them, which was to establish how two of them were alike and the third different from them. The client might say, for example: "My mother and my wife are alike in that they are both strong, dominant people, while my father tends to be quieter and more submissive." Kelly used any number of these comparisons which he judged to be sufficient to create a grid representing the matrix of the client's constructs used in defining the roles of the people with whom he or she relates. The finished picture is a part of the construed world of the person, the way he or she ascribes meaning to interpersonal relationships. This is apparent in Rowe's (1982) understanding of the ways in which people construe life and death.

This simple procedure has now been much enhanced by better methods of statistical analysis based on the correlations between the different elements of the grid (Bannister & Mair, 1968) and quicker and more informative feedback through the use of computer programmes (Shaw, 1980). Comparisons between groups of subjects is now possible. Unfortunately this often seems to involve the provision of standard constructs for all subjects, a procedure which to some extent contravenes the personal meanings of each subject's construed world. It is interesting that contravention of the same phenomenologically based assumption was made by most of the psychologists who used Q-sorts (Stephenson, 1953) to test the hypotheses about the self provided by Rogers. One exception was the Ideo-Q-Sort in which subjects created their own items for sorting as similar to or different from the self (Shlien, 1961). Q-sorts like that of Butler and Haigh (1954), on the other hand, forced subjects to try to communicate something of their own construed worlds in someone else's language. In Kelly's terms, they had to describe their own experience using someone else's constructs.

As well as the work stimulated by Rogers and Kelly, the phenomenological psychology group at Duquesne University has produced some interesting examples of psychological research which have relied on the cooperation of their subjects. Its members are aware of the importance of the experience of the subject as a source of data in a psychological enquiry (Giorgi, 1971). Let us take two phenomenological studies of learning as examples. The first report is of a dialogue between an experimenter and a subject in which the subject spoke of a learning experience she had had and the experimenter asked for clarification (Giorgi, 1975). In his analysis of this, Giorgi first read the entire verbatim report to get a sense of the whole. Next, he divided his subject's verbalisations into what appeared to him to be natural units and extracted the themes of these units. He then examined these phenomena in terms of his own interests: "What is learning?" and "How is learning accomplished?" Essential themes were then isolated by him at both the situational and general levels. This phenomenological reflection is a difficult and yet beguiling process; it must be carried out systematically and with rigour. It can produce not only research findings but also new working hypotheses. In this case some of the new hypotheses were: Would another person have obtained the same results? Does this structure of learning hold for many people? How many styles of learning are there?

This example involves analysis of one person's interpretations by another. However, such analysis can involve the interpretations of a group of subjects (Colaizzi, 1973). With his fifty subjects, he was interested in their experiences of a sample of ten different learning tasks, most of which were laboratory-based (for example, serial learning similar to that described in Chapter 2). The range of learning experiences of his subjects was quite wide, even if much of it involved tasks developed by psychologists for laboratory use. Among the many interesting perspectives on learning that Colaizzi obtained by having his subjects reflect on their experiences in the learning situation, one of the most thought provoking was the distinction they made between integrated experience-based learning and the mere acquisition of items of information.

The contributions made by the subjects to all of this work were made from within the traditional subject role. There is, however, at least one more step in the psychological enquiry with which subjects can help. That is in the organisation of what they have revealed of their experiences, in other words, the analysis of the data. When Fischer (1974) wrote of the phenomenological mode of researching "being anxious," he reported eliciting each subject's description of that experience. He refined it and clarified some of its themes, then checked them out with each subject to ensure that this process had not been a distorting one. The psychologist's reflection had to remain faithful to the interpretations of his subjects when using this Mutual Orientation Model of data collection. This employment of the subject as a data analyst has been the basis on which our research team developed the content analysis categories for our scales measuring uncertainty, helplessness, competence, and sociality (Viney & Westbrook, 1976; Viney & Westbrook, 1979; Westbrook & Viney, 1980). We also relied on a parallel assumption about the reflective capacity of experimenters and so examined the degree of agreement between panels of them using our categories (Viney, 1983c).

Subjects have been shown to be helpful collaborators as sources of data and as data analysts. A case has also been made for their involvement in the design of psychological research, especially to check out procedures which have been developed from the experimenter's viewpoint only (Kelly, 1969). Kelly also sees the subject as a source of hypotheses, as Giorgi does. If hypotheses are anticipatory experiences, then all experiencing people have hypotheses.

Each psychological enquiry can be viewed as consisting of these five sequentially occurring projects:

1. choosing the problem and setting the aims;

2. developing the hypotheses;

3. designing tests for the hypotheses,

   (i) selecting procedures, and

   (ii) sampling subjects;

4. analysing the resulting data; and

5. interpreting the findings in relation to the problem.

My students and I have found, by taking a personal construct perspective, that subjects can be productively involved in all of steps 2, 3, and 4 of the sequence. It probably should be psychologists who remain primarily responsible for defining the problem of the enquiry and interpreting the findings in the light of their specialised knowledge. In all of these other projects they might well seek the cooperation of their subjects.

Subjects are Assumed to be Construing People

In this Chapter I have examined some of the implications of assuming the subjects of psychological research to be construing people. This assumption or construct is compatible with the construct of reflexivity. What is appropriate for the psychologist is appropriate for the psychologist's subject. The distorting implications of the assumptions made by some traditional psychologists, for example, that subjects are not construers, have been further discussed. The similarities and differences between the personal construct approach and humanism have also been explored.

There has proved to be considerable support for my assumption that subjects are construing people. They are known to be active choosers, for example, in deciding whether to cooperate with the experimenter. They are seen to be interpreters when they strive to make sense of their experimental situation, relying on the cues provided by Orne's demand characteristics. Some of the problems which this involves have been noted, together with the disadvantages and advantages to the psychologist of working with subjects whom he or she perceives as reflective knowers. The disadvantages included subjects' suspiciousness and their evaluation-apprehension. The advantages included the still debated benefits of introspection.

The findings reviewed were then examined from a traditional psychological perspective, and its limiting view of subjects was revealed. Some recommendations about how to make these construing capacities of subjects part of the experiment -- since they form the central focus of the science of psychology -- were made. I have also presented some preliminary suggestions from the personal construct perspective. These have taken the form of data collections involving the cooperation of subjects, most of them arising, directly or indirectly, from the work of Kelly, as well as Rogers and Giorgi. It has become apparent that subjects are able to make a much greater collaborative contribution to psychological research than they are currently making. It is time, now, to leave

the subjects of psychological experiments and to turn to those other important
people in psychological research, the experimenters.

References

Adair, J.G.   (1973). The human subject: The social psychology of the
   psychological experiment. Boston: Little, Brown.

Argyris, C. (1968). Some unintended consequences of rigorous research.
   Psychological Bulletin, 70, 185-197.

Bakan, D. (1967). On method. San Francisco: Jossey-Bass.

Baloff, N. & Becker, S.W. (1967).   On the futillity of aggregating individual
   learning curves. Psychological Reports, 20, 182-191.

Bannister, D. (1966). Psychology as an exercise in paradox. Bulletin of the
   British Psychological Society, 19, 21-26.

Bannister, D. & Mair, J.M.M. (1968). The evaluation of personal constructs.
   London: Academic Press.

Bickman, L. & Henchy, T. (Eds.) (1972). Beyond laboratory - field research in
   social psychology (pp.110-119). New York: McGraw-Hill.

Bloch, J. (1965). The challenge of response sets. New York: Appleton-
   Century-Crofts.

Boch, R.D. (1975). Multivariate statistical methods in behavioural research. New
   York: McGraw-Hill.

Boring, E.G. (1953). A history of introspection. Psychological Bulletin, 50,
   169-189.

Buhler, C. (1965). Some observations on the psychology of the third force.
   Journal of Humanistic Psychology, 5, 54.

77

Buhler, C. & Allen, M. (1972). Introduction to humanistic psychology. Monterey, California: Brooks/Cole.

Burt, C. (1962). The concept of consciousness. British Journal of Psychology, 53, 229-242.

Butler, J.M. & Haigh, G.V. (1954). Changes in the relation between self-concepts and ideal-concepts consequent upon client-centred counselling. In C.R. Rogers & R.F. Dymond (Eds.) Psychotherapy and personality change (pp.16-32). Chicago: University of Chicago Press.

Campbell, D.T. (1969). Prospective: Artifact and control. In R. Rosenthal and R.L. Rosnow (Eds.) Artifact in behavioural research (pp.212-220). New York: Academic Press.

Cantril, H. (1967). A fresh look at human design. In J.F.T. Bugental (Ed.) Challenges of humanistic psychology (pp.13-18). New York: McGraw-Hill.

Cardno, J.A. (1966). Psychology: Human, humanistic, humane. Journal of Humanistic Psychology, 6, 278-298.

Child, L.L. (1973). Humanistic psychology and the research tradition. New York: Wiley.

Colaizzi, P.F. (1973). Reflection and research in psychology: A phenomeno-logical study of learning. Dubuque, Iowa: Kendall Hunt.

Criswell, J.H. (1958). The psychologist as perceiver. In R. Taguiri & L. Petrullo (Eds.) Person perception and interpersonal behaviour (pp.36-44). Stanford: Stanford University Press.

Danziger, K. (1985). The origins of the psychological experiment as a social institution. American Psychologist, 40, 133-140.

DeCharms, R. (1968). Personal causation. New York: Academic Press.

Edwards, A.L. (1957). The social desirability variable. New York: Dryden.

Epstein, Y.M.; Suedfield, P. & Silverstein, S.J. (1973). The experimental contract: Subjects' expectations of and reactions to some behaviours of experimenters. American Psychologist, 28, 212-221.

Farr, J.L. & Seaver, W.B. (1975). Stress and discomfort in psychological research: Subject perception of experimental procedures. American Psychologist, 30, 770-773.

Fischer, W.F. (1974). On the phenomenological mode of researching "being anxious." Journal of Phenomenological Psychology, 4, 405-423.

Fischer, C.T. (1976). The meaning of phenomenological psychology. A.P.A Division of Philosophical Psychology Newsletter, Spring.

Frank, J.D. (1973). Persuasion and healing. Baltimore: Johns Hopkins University Press.

Freeman, E.L. & Viney, L.L. (1977). Patients' initial expectations of the therapist role. Journal of Community Psychology, 5, 372-379.

Giorgi, A. (1971). The experience of the subject as a source of data in a psychological experiment. In A. Giorgi, W.F. Fischer & R. Von Eckartsberg (Eds.) Duquesne Studies in Phenomenological Psychology. Pittsburgh, Pa.: Duquesne University Press, 1, 50-57.

Giorgi, A. (1975). An application of phenomenological method in psychology. In A. Giorgi, C.T. Fischer and E.L. Murray (Eds.) Duquesne Studies in Phenomenological Psychology. Pittsburgh, Pa.: Duquesne University Press, 2, 82-103.

Hilgard, E.R. (1965). Hypnotic suggestibility. New York: Harcourt Brace and World.

Hilgard, J. (1970). Personality and hypnosis. Chicago: University of Chicago Press.

Hitt, W. (1969). Two models of man. American Psychologist, 24, 651-658.

Hull, C.L. (1933). Hypnosis and suggestibility: An experimental approach. New York: Appleton-Century-Crofts.

John, I.D. (1984). Experimental subjects' impressions of that experience. Bulletin of the Australian Psychological Society, 6, 7-8.

Jones, E.E. & Davis, K.E. (1965). From acts to dispositions. In L. Berkowitz (Ed.) Advances in experimental social psychology, Vol. 2, (pp.62-75). New York: Academic Press.

Kelly, G.A. (1955). The psychology of personal constructs. New York: Norton.

Kelly, G.A. (1969). Humanistic methodology in psychological research. Journal of Humanistic Psychology, 9, 53-65.

Köstler, A. (1969). Ethical issues involved in influencing the mind. In Köstler, A. et al. The ethics of change. Toronto: Canadian Broadcasting Organization.

Kuenzli, A.E. (Ed.) (1959). The phenomenological problem. New York: Harper.

Landfield, A.W. (1970). High priests, reflexivity and congruency of client-therapist personal construct systems. British Journal of Medical Psychology, 43, 207-212.

Lazlo, J.P. & Rosenthal, R. (1971). Subject dogmatism, experimental status and experimenter expectancy effect. Personality, 1, 11 - 23.

Lester, D. (1969). The subject as a source of bias in psychological research. Journal of General Psychology, 81, 237-248.

McGuire, W.J. (1969). Suspiciousness of experimenter's intent. In R. Rosenthal and R.L. Rosnow (Eds.) Artifact in behavioural research (pp.13-57). New York: Academic Press

Mair, J.M.M. (1970). Experimenting with individuals. British Journal of Medical Psychology, 43, 245-256.

Mair, J.M.M. (1977). The community of self. In D. Bannister (Ed.) New perspectives in personal construct theory (pp.96-105). London: Academic Press.

Marquis, P. (1973). Experimenter-subject interaction as a function of authoritarianism and response set. Journal of Personality and Social Psychology, 25, 289-296.

Meadows, C.M. (1975). The phenomenology of joy: An empirical investigation. Psychological Reports, 37, 39-54.

Mischel, W. (1977). On the future of personality assessment. American Psychologist, 32, 246-254.

Misiak, H. & Sexton, V.S. (1973). Phenomenological, existential and humanistic psychologies: A historical survey. New York: Grune & Stratton.

Musante, G. & Anker, J.M. (1972). E's presence: Effect on S's performance. Psychological Reports, 30, 903-904.

Orne, M.T. (1962). On the social psychology of the psychological experiment with particular reference to demand characteristics and their implications. American Psychologist, 17, 776-783.

Orne, M.T. (1969). Demand characteristics and the concept of quasi-controls. In R. Rosenthal and R.L. Rosnow (Eds.) Artifact in behavioural research (pp.143-179). New York: Academic Press.

Overall, J.E. & Klett, C.J. (1972). Applied multivariate analysis. New York: McGraw-Hill.

Penner, L.A. et al. (1973). Obedience as a function of experimenter competence. Memory and Cognition, 1, 241-245.

Perrot, L.A. (1977). Research on research: The human dimension. Journal of Phenomenological Psychology, 7, 148-171.

Pierce, A.H. (1908). The subconscious again. Journal of Philosophical Psychology, Science and Methodology, 5, 264-271.

Richards, F. (1972). The unknown subject. Journal of Humanistic Psychology, 12, 22-23.

Riecken, H.W. (1962). A programme for research on experiments in social psychology. In N.F. Washburne (Ed.) Decisions, values and groups. New York: Pergamon, 2, 25-41.

Rinn, J.L. (1966). Dimensions of group interaction: The co-operative analysis of idiosyncratic descriptions of training groups. Education and Psychological Measurement. 26, 343-362.

Rogers, C.R. (1959). A theory of therapy, personality and interpersonal relationships as developed in a client-centred framework. In S. Koch (Ed.) Psychology: A study of a science. New York: McGraw-Hill, 3.

Rogers, C.R. (1961). On becoming a person. Boston: Houghton Mifflin.

Rosenberg, M.J. (1965). When dissonance fails: On eliminating evaluation apprehension from attitude measurement. Journal of Personality and Social Psychology, 1, 28-42.

Rosenberg, M.J. (1969). Conditions and consequences of evaluation apprehension. In R. Rosenthal and R.L. Rosnow (Eds.) Artifact in behavioural research (pp.280-349). New York: Academic Press.

Rosenthal, R. (1967). Covert communicationn in the psychological experiment. Psychological Bulletin, 67, 356-367.

Rosenthal, R. (1969). Interpersonal expectations: Effects of the experimenter's hypothesis. In R. Rosenthal and R.L. Rosnow (Eds.) Artifact in behavioural research (pp.181-277). New York: Academic Press.

Rosenthal, R. (1976). Experimenter effects in behavioural research. New York: Appleton-Century-Crofts.

Rosenthal, R. & Rosnow, R.L. (Eds.) (1969). Artifact in behavioural research. N.Y.: Academic Press.

Rosenzweig, S. (1933). The experimental situation as a psychological problem. Psychological Review, 40, 337-354.

Rowe, D. (1982). The construction of life and death. New York: Wiley.

Salmon, P. (1979). Children as social beings. In P. Stringer & D. Bannister (Eds.) Constructs of sociality and individuality (pp.8-16). London:

83

Academic Press.

Salmon, P. (1980). Coming to know. London: Routledge & Kegan Paul.

Savin, H.B. (1973). Professors and psychological researchers: Conflicting values in conflicting roles. Cognition, 2, 147-149.

Schafer, R. (1954). Psychoanalytic interpretation in Rorschach testing. New York: Grune & Stratton, 1954.

Schultz, D.P. (1969). The human subject in psychological research. Psychological Bulletin, 72, 214-228.

Shaw, M.L.G. (1980). On becoming a personal scientist. London: Academic Press.

Sigall, H., Aronson, E. & Van Hoose, T. (1970). The co-operative subject: Myth or reality. Journal of Experimental and Social Psychology, 6, 1-10.

Stephenson, W. (1953). The study of behaviour: Q technique and its methodology. Chicago: University of Chicago Press.

Stricker, L.J.M., Messick, S. & Jackson, D. (1969). Evaluating deception in psychological research. Psychological Bulletin, 71, 343 - 351.

Stout, G.F. (1938). A manual of psychology. London: University Tutorial Press.

Sullivan, D.S. & Deiker, T.E. (1973). Subject-experimenter perception of ethical issues in human research. American Psychologist, 28, 587-591.

Tolman, E. (1938). The determiners of behaviour at a choice point. Psychological Review, 45, 1-41.

Viney, L.L. (1980). Transitions. Sydney: Cassell.

Viney, L.L. (1981). Content analysis: A research tool for community psychologists. American Journal of Community Psychology, 9, 269-281.

Viney, L.L. (1983a). Images of illness. Malabar, Florida: Krieger.

Viney, L.L. (1983b). Psychological reactions of young people to unemployment. Youth and Community, 14, 457-474.

Viney, L.L. (1983c). The assessment of psychological states through content analysis of verbal communications. Psychological Bulletin, 94, 542-563.

Viney, L.L. (1985). Physical illness: A guidebook for the kingdom of the sick. In E. Button (Ed.) Personal construct theory and mental health. Beckenham: Croom Helm.

Viney, L.L. & Tych, A.M. (1985). Content analysis scales to measure psychosocial maturity in the elderly. Journal of Personality Assessment, 49, 311-317.

Viney, L.L. & Westbrook, M.T. (1976). Cognitive anxiety: A method of content analysis for verbal samples. Journal of Personality Assessment, 40, 140-150.

Viney, L.L. & Westbrook, M.T. (1979). Sociality: A content analysis for verbalisations. Social Behaviour and Personality, 7, 129-137.

Viney, L.L. & Westbrook, M.T. (1981). Measuring patients' experienced quality of life: The application of content analysis scales in health care. Community Health Studies, 5, 45-52.

Viney, L.L. & Westbrook, M.T. (1982). Patterns of anxiety in the chronically ill. British Journal of Medical Psychology, 55, 87-95.

Weber, S.J. & Cook, T.D. (1972). Subject effects in laboratory research. Psychological Bulletin, 77, 273-295.

Westbrook, M.T. & Viney, L.L. (1980). Measuring peoples' perceptions of themselves as origins or pawns. Journal of Personality Assessment, 44, 157-166.

Wilson, D.W. & Downerstein, E. (1976). Legal and ethical aspects of non-reactive social research. American Psychologist, 31, 765-773.

Zimbardo, P.G. (1973). The mind is a formidable gaoler: A Pirandellian prison. The New York Times Magazine, April 8, (pp. 38-60).

Zoble, E.J. & Lehman, R.S. (1969). Interaction of subject and experimenter expectancy effects in a tone length discrimination task. Behavioural Science, 14, 357-363.

CHAPTER 4

EXPERIMENTERS AS CONSTRUING PEOPLE

Do we make the same assumptions about the experimenters in psychological

enquiries as we make about ourselves?

Do we define what the experimenters do or do they?

Why do experimenters participate in our enquiries?

Are we making the best use of our experimenters?

Could our experimenters be better trained? If so, how?

I have always thought of experimenters as being very important to psychological research. We psychologists seem to spend more of our precious research funds on research assistants to fill this role than our colleagues in physics or chemistry do. Whether the experimenter role is important or not is one of the questions to be answered in this chapter. I shall distinguish here between experimenters, who actually collect the data, and psychologists, who develop and control the research programmes of psychology. This chapter is mainly about experimenters, but, because the two roles are often combined in one person, I shall sometimes relate my comments to psychologists as well.

On reading this paragraph I find that I have been unable to resist, even in one of its first few sentences, making the assumption of this discussion: that experimenters are construing people. The empirical evidence supporting this assumption and some of the implications of it will be examined within the framework of personal construct psychology. As this was the framework used when discussing subjects of psychological experiments in Chapter 3, the reader will be able to make a comparison of experimenter and subject roles.

As the Subject, so the Experimenter

Reflexivity must work both ways. If the subject's behaviour is viewed in terms of stimulus and response alone, then so must the experimenter's and psychologist's be (Straus, 1966). A psychologist cannot present a picture of the person which conflicts with his or her own observed behaviour (Bannister, 1970a). Actually, Skinner (1972) has been able to account for his own researching behaviour quite well in stimulus-response terms. This is not the case with many experimenters, however. In studies of psychological motives, the assumption is often made that the motives of experimenter and subject are different (Brandt, 1971), as in the controversial study of obedience (Milgram, 1963). The law of parsimony requires that, where possible, one motive should be ascribed to the behaviour of both. What about curiosity to account for both Milgram, the researcher, and his apparently obedient subjects? This is compatible with the personal construct view of man as scientist. Might not both experimenter and subject be behaving in such a way as to increase their future range of alternatives?

This lack of reflexivity appears to be a result of pseudo-objectivity (Deutscher, 1983).

> "If I explain I have no will of my own, that people are influencing me in subtle and mysterious ways, you'll accuse me of being paranoid and direct me to a psychotherapist. If I put on a white lab coat, and I assert that you have no will of your own, and that your actions and experience can be manipulated, predicted and controlled, then I am recognised as a scientific psychologist, and honoured. This is most peculiar."
>
> (Jourard, 1968, p.1)

I agree with Jourard: it is peculiar. It makes me want to return very quickly to the view of experimenters as active construers.

Active Choosers

Just as some of the natural activity of subjects is described as "subject error," so is some of the natural activity of experimenters described as "experimenter bias." Five sources of such bias have been defined (Barber, 1972). They include experimenters treating subjects in different ways and experimenters fudging results. In addition, there are the effects of the personal attributes of the experimenters, the errors made by experimenters in the analysis of data, and experimenters falsifying data when it is difficult to collect. This depressing list may seem unduly suspicious of experimenters. However, much of it seems appropriate when their possible motives are considered.

They may be considerably influenced by the prospect of keeping their jobs as experimenters or even by the prospect of promotion. The research programme which finds support for its hypotheses may have a better chance of refunding than that which does not. These "in-order-to" motives hold for researchers, too. The choice of problems by psychologists is often determined by cost, confirmability, and conformability (Webb, 1961). Of the last two determinants, the confirmability applies to the hypotheses and the conformability to the psychologists. The world of research psychologists is a highly competitive one (Reif, 1961). Experimenters, like subjects, have a stake in maintaining their self-esteem during an enquiry, and this may well affect their "error"-proneness. No researcher or experimenter was ever uninvolved in the results of his or her experiment (Roe, 1961; Kelly, 1969). "Science would be far less advanced than she is if the passionate desires of individuals to get their own faiths confirmed had been kept out of the game..." (James, 1948, p.62).

Experimenters can vary also in whether they choose to disclose themselves actively to their subjects: their aims, their interests, as well as their motives. Such self-disclosure may have effects on the subsequent actions of subjects during an enquiry (Jourard, 1971). Subjects are, for example, more likely to disclose themselves -- in other words, to show more candour with their experimenters. There is a more mutual orientation, in the terms of symbolic interactionism (Mead, 1962). There is also more sharing of motives, from the perspective of Schütz (1967). Subjects are likely to change their perceptions of experimenters who have been candid with them. More importantly subjects have been shown actually to alter the responses which happen to be currently of interest to the psychologist after experimenter self-disclosure. Testees gave different responses on standardised tests, including personality inventories like those described in Chapter 2. They also showed faster mastery of a paired associate learning task after self-disclosure by the experimenter (Jourard, 1971).

Experimenters appear to be fairly active when they are, as it is said, "running" experiments. They communicate with subjects using both verbal and nonverbal symbols (Rosenthal, 1967). Something of the range of their activities can be seen in the list of experimenter behaviours used in the study referred to in Chapter 3 (Epstein, Suedfield & Silverstein, 1973). Subjects thought, for example, that experimenters should describe the experiment to them, give any necessary warnings, indicate the duration, place, and time of the experiment, state its purpose, and describe what will be done with the data. And all this before the experiment starts! Some possible experimental procedures have also been listed (Farr & Seaver, 1975). They include subjects being given an electric shock, asked to talk in front of others, and told that they have homosexual tendencies. These procedures indicate what a probing and prying role that of the psychological experimenter can become. This is not inappropriate in one sense, since it is the job of the experimenter, by definition, to manipulate variables. Physicists realise that by probing into it they have an effect on the world they are studying (Shotter, 1970). Psychologists are, however, often surprisingly naive about the full effects of their manipulations.

This naiveté of some psychologists about the consequences of some of their actions also holds about their mythmaking. "Schizophrenia" provides an excellent example of such a myth (Bannister, 1976). The main finding of behaviourally based studies of schizophrenia has been that samples of people labelled as "schizophrenic" yield strikingly large variances for nearly every variable measured. This justifies a description of the concept as an "intellectual ragbag." The concept of "schizophrenia" may be equated with "madness," that is, it is a symbol we choose to use to account for the unaccountable. Psychologists and psychiatrists have developed this construct by which we hope to make sense of these "mad" people (Szasz, 1973). Unfortunately, the construct does not do its job very well. First, it is too loose, that is, it embraces too much of our lived world to be useful. Second, it may also be easily invalidated by making sense of "schizophrenic" behaviour (Sullivan, 1953; Laing, 1961; Haley, 1963).

Interpreters

Making myths is, of course, a way of construing experience. It is not a good way because myths, when they do not accurately represent the world, may not serve well to predict future events. There are, however, occasions on which they do, and these can be very dangerous for the mythmaker. I am thinking of those occasions when one person's myth becomes accepted by others, and in consequence they act so as to fulfill the predictions of that myth. This can easily happen to social scientists who may create a "reality" from their theories (Schütz, 1953). The "reality" is supposed to be self-determining, but actually the scientist has much control over it (Williams, 1977). The work on experimenter expectancy effects demonstrates this (Rosenthal, 1976). This work also serves to show that the experimenter of psychological experiments is an interpreter and a creator of meaning.

The experimenter expectancy effect consists of the expectancies experimenters have of how their subjects will respond and of their own effects on the subjects' behaviour. The expectancies or interpretations of the experimenters may determine to some extent the results of their research (Rosenthal, 1976). It is appropriate, I think, to describe the details of Rosenthal's first experiment (Rosenthal & Fode, 1961). In it, ten undergraduate psychology students served as experimenters, and their subjects were students enrolled in an introductory psychology course. The experimenters were told that they were helping to develop a test for empathy and that they would get practice in duplicating experimental results. They were instructed to obtain ratings of photographs from their subjects. These instructions to the experimenters were identical in every way except that five of them were told that their subjects would average a +5 rating for the apparently neutral photographs and the other five were given the expectancy of an average rating of -5. When the rating results became available, the average ratings of the first group of experiments were clustered around +5 and the average ratings of the second were much lower. In fact, the two distributions of ratings did not overlap.

There have been many replications of this experimenter expectancy effect with different kinds of subjects. At the infrahuman level, experimenters observed the (albeit limited) behaviour of a sample of planaria (Cordaro & Ison, 1963). For half of the worms, the experimenters were led to expect much movement; for the other half, the same experimenters were led to expect little. The worms, insofar as anyone could tell, were identical. However, the experimenters reported twice as many head turns and three times as many body turns for the first set of worms as for the second. This experimenter expectancy effect has also been demonstrated with animals further up the phylogenetic scale, and therefore with a greater range of behaviour -- for example, with that trusted laboratory staple, the albino rat (Rosenthal & Fode, 1961). Since I have defined psychology, for the purposes of this discussion, as the study of people, I shall not pursue such studies here.

The number of experimenter expectancy effect experiments which have been carried out with human subjects is too large to review in this chapter. Rosenthal himself reviewed studies in seven different areas of psychology -- animal learning, human learning and ability, psychophysical judgements, reaction time studies, projective techniques, laboratory interviews, and person perception -- collected from twenty-nine different laboratories (Rosenthal, 1969; 1976). I have participated in a demonstration of the effect in a psychophysiological experiment, in fact, on the electroencephalogram and electromyogram responses of subjects which are not usually under their control (Clarke, Michie, Andreasen, Viney & Rosenthal, 1976). The results of such studies may not have demonstrated conclusively an experimenter expectancy effect (Barber & Silver, 1968). Yet there does appear to be enough evidence to say that the effect may occur.

Some of the experiments can also be criticised as involving very simple, concrete expectancies. What happens when the constructs of the psychologist are more complex, as they usually are? Research in hypnosis provides one answer. A complex set of relationships between hypnotiseability and various types of conformity had been established (Rosenhahn, 1967). Before the new experimenter tried to replicate the earlier experimenter's work, she was shown the pattern of correlations that he had obtained but with the sign of every correlation coefficient reversed. Her subjects' subsequent hypnotic behaviour clearly showed the effects of this reversal. Both experimenters were acting towards the objects of their worlds according to the different meanings they held for them, and what different effects emerged!

Many experimenter and subject factors affect the appearance of an experimenter expectancy effect (Rosenthal, 1976). A subject's expectancies, for example, may preclude its appearance. Also, early data returns may affect the experimenter's expectancies. It is also interesting that offering the experimenters high incentives to produce the effect in fact reduced it (Rosenthal et al., 1964). We must look at the meaning this had for the experimenters. "Several of them used the term 'payola', suggesting that they felt that the investigators were bribing them to get good data..." (Rosenthal, 1976, p.218). Other relevant factors include sex of experimenter and subject, their personality traits, and, of course, the status of the experimenter. These last two factors were combined in a study already reported in Chapter 3. High scorers on Rokeach's Dogmatism Scale were found to be more susceptible than low scorers to the effect of the expectancies of their experimenters (Laszlo & Rosenthal, 1971).

Whether the expectancies are conveyed from experimenter to subject by unintentional or intentional communication on the part of the experimenter is not yet clear. What is clear, from the personal construct approach, is that the intention of both subject and experimenter is meaningfully to anticipate the events involved. In the psychophysiological study cited above (Clarke et al., 1976), we included, as a moderator variable, a measure of perceived locus of control (Rotter, 1966). This measure differentiates between people who experience a primarily internal locus of control -- that is, who expect to have an influence on what happens to them and to wield that influence meaningfully -- and those who have a primarily external locus of control -- that is, who expect to have no influence over their own lives and see themselves as the flotsam or jetsam of fate. The research relating to this construct-based concept has been reviewed by Lefcourt (1976; 1981) and Phares (1976). Our finding was not that the locus of control expectancies of either experimenter or subject alone permitted the experimenter's hypotheses to affect the subject's response, but that the similarity of the expectancies or constructs of each of them was important. I shall suggest that a sharing of lived worlds is what is occurring in this experiment -- a mutual orientation -- and leave further discussion of this effect until Chapter 5.

Reflective Knowers

I would like now to address some of the issues engaged by regarding experimenters as reflective knowers. But what I found when I examined reports of experimenters in psychological studies is that they are rarely engaged in that capacity. The ability of experimenters to reflect on their own experiences is not often used, especially in studies which employ the Reactive Orientation Model of data collection. In fact, the experimenter role which is preferred, wherever possible, is a sterile one. At least, that is how it is presented in the literature. We may suspect, from the findings reviewed in this chapter, that these reports are not always accurate.

The experimenter is not, in actuality, powerful, even when he or she is employed with the Experimenter Orientation Model. This is because it is not the experimenter but the psychologist who defines the experimental situation. As far as I can ascertain, there is only one way in which experimenters have been asked to act as reflective knowers. That is when they are asked to be critically aware of the methods they use. This is an important function, since it is one which may be said to distinguish our work as psychologists from the hypothesis testing about people carried out by every woman and man in the street. Even in this way, however, the considerable skills (especially interpersonal skills) possessed by experimenters because they are construing people are barely considered. Reports by experimenters that the experiment is not running in a standardised manner are not, I would guess, often encouraged.

Naive experimenters are preferred. Yet, experimenters who do not reflect on their own experience could not maintain a sense of identity. Now it is true that adults, at least, who are called upon to fill the experimenter role have usually already established some sense of their own identity and enjoy other experiences through which to maintain it. What may happen in that role, then, is this. Because experimenters -- if reports are to be believed -- refrain from reflection, they never come to associate their identity with the experimental situation. Experiential reports have been collected from experimenters in Rosenthal-type experiments. From phenomenological analyses of these reports and from the observations of the rituals of the psychological laboratory, the conclusions of the researcher are similar to mine. "It is precisely in losing his identity as a particular human personality that the experimenter gains his identity as a proper experimenter" (O'Donovan, 1968, p.143). The identity of that "proper experimenter," however, is so meaningless and so limiting of his or her capacities to know reflectively that it, as well as the role of the subject, might well be filled by the robots to which I referred in Chapter 2.

Some Traditional Psychological Perspectives

Of course such suggestions about robot experimenters have been being made from within traditional psychology for some time (Miller, Bregman & Norman, 1965). Computers can go much farther than merely running experiments. They can be designed to generate functional models and draw up and carry out experiments which will compare the hypotheses of one model with those of another (Wolfendale, 1969; Guetzkow, Kotler & Schultz, 1972). The myths and assumptions of psychologists will still, however, be perpetuated, since they will have been built into the software used with these computers. Let us turn back to the simpler suggestion, that of computer as data collector. It may well reduce so-called experimenter bias. But the psychology which results must be recognised as a person-and-machine psychology and must take as its aim the definition of the relationship between people and computers. This is a far cry from a psychologist's view of his or her work as a process by which one person becomes acquainted with another person (Hudson, 1972).

The argument for computers as experimenters is, in fact, the logical end point of the argument for minimal contact between experimenter and subject which is made by many psychologists (Plutchik, 1968). If contact has to occur, let it not be effective. It is surprising to find a social psychologist supporting this myth (Rosenthal, 1976). Rosenthal has admitted that some experiments require human interaction and has tried to specify ways of restricting the cues available to subject and experimenter without apparently realising that the people in these roles will create meaning to fill his desired vacuum (Orne, 1969).

Blind procedures are, of course, another variation on this theme (Plutchik, 1968). It may seem plausible to some to assume that if an experimenter does not know whether the subject has been assigned to an experimental or to a control group, he or she cannot have expectancies about how the subject should act. Yet, a person does not passively accept such a state of affairs, but continues to try to make sense of what is happening. This was brought home to me in an evaluation I was making of the effects of the introduction of speech therapy into the programmes of institutionalised retarded children (Viney, 1972). It was apparent to the nurses who looked after them that certain children were involved in the study. However, I was at pains to ensure that they did not know whether any particular child was working on speech or spending time in a control condition. Nor could the severely speech impaired children tell them. Yet the nurses formed their own impressions of who was in which group, guessing with no better than chance accuracy. The results indicated that speech therapy was, unfortunately, not associated with improvements in the children's speech. Yet the constructs of the nurses were. My study had proved to be a replication in another type of institution of the findings of Pygmalion in the Classroom (Rosenthal & Jacobson, 1968; Rosenthal, 1973).

Another social psychologist concluded from what he refers to as his examination of the experimenter as a "stimulus object", that we must test our generalisations from one experimenter, or a few, to a population of experimenters (McGuigan, 1963). Yet another suggestion from this work is that we learn to specify techniques for controlling variables. The hope is that they might be like the "quasi-controls" of Orne for the effects of demand characteristics, allowing experimenters to use their capacities more effectively. The third recommendation requires the building up of a bank of knowledge about how experimenters affect subjects in a variety of experimental situations. This last suggestion appeals to me, although I am not sure how we should select our sample experimental situations. I would add again here, however, the recommendation which I made with regard to so-called subject error. These experimenter effects should be accepted as some of the essential phenomena of psychology and examined in the context of psychological enquiries with the tools for multivariate analyses which are now available (Boch, 1975).

Some suggestions have also been made about how experimenters might be more appropriately trained (Barber, 1972; Rosenthal, 1976). They recognise to varying extents the experimenters' capabilities as construing people. Experimenters are exhorted to be aware of variations in their own actions during an experiment. This is good advice. More frequently, however, the cry is for closer checks on experimenters by others. This is necessary where there is concern that they are "fudging" results or falsifying data. But many of these "errors" occur without experimenter awareness. A much more effective and radical response to this problem requires a reduced emphasis on positive results in training experimenters (Barber, 1972). Less importance given to "predicting correctly" generally in psychology might release both researchers and experimenters for a more fruitful exploration and description of their construed world.

Since experimenter expectancy effects provide some of the best demonstrations available that experimenters are construing people, it is necessary to examine the traditional psychological perspective on how psychologists should deal with them. When they are conceptualised as "experimenter artifacts" they can be "controlled" by some of the measures noted already. For example, experimenters can be kept blind to the purpose of the experiment... Well, researchers try to do so! Careful observation of experimenters' behaviour, with correction where necessary, has been suggested. The addition of experimenter expectancy control groups to the experimental design has also been proposed. There is, however, concern about the ethical implications of the deception necessary. Some psychologists even go to the lengths of suggesting that a control group of experimenters "with no expectations" should be run (Barber & Silver, 1968). If my assumption that experimenters are actively construing people holds, the only good experimenters for these psychologists would be dead experimenters!

The development of a job role of professional experimenter or data collector in psychology, as in other sciences, has also been recommended (Rosenthal, 1976). This could certainly lead to more competent and less biased experimenters. Yet they would still be personally involved and, so, striving to make sense of their situation. They could be trained, however, so that they and others come to evaluate their work in terms of well-run experiments rather than in terms of the confirmation of hypotheses. They could learn to attend to more of their interpretation of the experiment than they now do. Their interpersonal sensitivities, too, could be better developed (Sullivan, 1937). They would be, for example, better able to elicit and reflect on the experience-based reports of their subjects and so better able to relate them to their behaviour. This goal would involve experimenters in being better able to develop a relationship of trust with subjects than is now the case. They would also be better able to "listen" to their communications and to clarify their interpersonally shared constructs. We have seen that subjects' introspective reports are still used in psychology. Yet, there is no reason to believe that they, at the present time, provide useful data. Subjects in a verbal conditioning experiment were informed about the details of the reinforcement procedure (Levy, 1967). When they were later directly asked whether they were aware of them, only a quarter of the group replied that they were.

The Personal Construct Perspective

The picture of experimenters which has emerged in this chapter is far from a personal construct perspective on people, perhaps even further than that for subjects of psychological experiments proved to be. An extension of the experimenter role based on personal construct psychology should now be provided. The first aspect of the new role that comes to mind is the capitalisation on the interpersonal sensitivity of experimenters as construing people. This has been developed, to some extent, in the experimenter role of participant observer (Bruyn, 1966; Bogdan & Taylor, 1975). The effects of their ability to enter the lived world of another are more fully explored in Chapter 5. Let us now turn to a more basic attribute of these interpreting people, their ability to trust their own experiencing and, when appropriate, that of their subjects. Exercising this ability should also open up some new horizons for the planning of data collections, as it has done in the content analysis scales I mentioned in Chapter 3. Experimenters are trained to use the scoring categories, and their interjudge reliability is calculated (Viney, 1983).

Personal construct psychologists have argued, as has William James, for the benefits of strong personal involvement in the experiment on the part of experimenters. Detached experimenters do not exist. If they did, they would not be good for psychology. The necessary commitment, openness to what emerges, and perseverance in the face of the inevitable obstacles is only brought about through personal involvement. Involvement with subjects in the experimental situation is also necessary, because without it -- that is, with experimenter detachment -- evaluation apprehension is likely to be produced in these subjects. This may be the least of the resulting problems. At worst, the psychological enquiry is unproductive or misleading.

There are senses in which experimenters are involved, whether they like it or not, to the point of being subjects of their own research. Experimenters can, as O'Donovan (1968) has demonstrated, be themselves a primary source of psychological data, that is, by reflecting on their own interpretations. Experimenters, if the personal construct view of people is a valid one, will be continually looking for new hypotheses and not just seeking to confirm old ones. According to Schütz (1967), they will be acting according to plan. If the experimenter and research psychologist are not one and the same, the experimenter is much closer to what is happening in the experiment. He or she can therefore more easily find new ways of making sense of it, that is, of practising constructive alternativism. The full extension of this experimenter role requires experimenters who maximise their interaction with the phenomena of interest (Kelly, 1969). They can do so by collaborating with their subjects. They can observe everything that happens and not just that which involves the designated variables. They can serve themselves as subjects. Finally, they can try to interpret the interpretations of their subjects.

These recommendations are based on a view of the person as a construer. There is yet another experimenter role, akin to this role in its reliance on the experimenter as a construer. That, put simply, is one of pattern recognition. "Science is the activity of putting order into our experience" (Bronowski, 1952). The main aim of psychologists is to perceive patterns (or relationships, if you will) in the psychological phenomena which they encounter (Rogers, 1968). Social psychologists, too, see this as an important goal (Harré, 1974). Piaget is one psychologist who has actively pursued such an aim in his work on intelligence (Piaget, 1930) to which I referred in Chapter 2. Although some personal construct psychologists are critical of him for not remaining within the construed world of his subjects, others perceive him as searching for the essential structures of experience, that is, for constructs. The effect of Piaget's approach has been to undermine the old myth of intelligence as a collection of mental powers, a step made possible by his phenomenological approach. Cognitive science has grown from these beginnings.

105

Within this personal construct approach (Dreyfus, 1982), it must be remembered that the patterns observed may be somewhat different from those of traditional psychology (Fodor, 1968). They are not necessarily patterns linking cause(s) with effect(s). They can involve rational explanation in which reasons for actions, such as justification, signalling intention, or classification, can serve to identify patterns without any implications of causation (Toulmin, 1970). This is the function of personal constructs (Mischel, 1964). Other ways of elucidating patterns are currently being explored. One such method is an old one indeed. This is Aristotle's dialectical reasoning through dialogues which explore opposites (Rychlak, 1970). Many different kinds of patterns may emerge.

The phenomenological method of reflection described in Chapter 1 of this book can be put to good use by psychological experimenters who are active construers and who know and can critically reflect, using constructs, on what and how they know. We can see illustrations of such uses in the examples of research carried out by phenomenological psychologists examined in Chapter 3 (Giorgi, 1975; Perrot, 1977). Giorgi's approach involves initially reading an experientially based protocol to get a general sense of it and then breaking it up into what he calls natural units. Those units, in themselves, constitute a description of the phenomenon in which he was interested. In the second example, Perrot interviewed three experimenters, conducted thematic analyses of their transcripts and then integrated them to form a coherent description of more general phenomena. Both psychologists/experimenters employed a method of content analysis in which the content was based on the reports of their subjects, making the most of their own ability to listen and construe.

Experimenters should learn to be good listeners. "Good" I mean in the sense of appearing to subjects to be attentive to them, but also accurate and perceptive. They may even learn to carry out phenomenological reductions (Woodhouse, 1984). These are the skills which personal construct psychologists have advocated. They are not necessarily easy for experimenters to develop. If I were training people for the role of professional experimenter, as suggested by Rosenthal, I would provide role play of the two roles of the experimental situation, to yield experiences through which these skills could be developed. This is, after all, how interpersonal skills are developed in psychodrama (Schonke, 1975). Role play would also provide an opportunity for role reversal (Moreno, 1969), which would give experimenters a much more vivid and personally meaningful understanding of what it is like to be subjects. I would also have advocated the actual experience of being a subject in an experiment, but for the fact that most of us have been subjects when we were students in introductory psychology courses. The current recollections of myself and my colleagues of those experiences suggest that they were somewhat threatening and that, as personal construct psychology would predict, we have therefore not allowed them to remain a part of our construed worlds. Certainly, experimenters should undertake their subject's role before beginning any experiment they are going to conduct.

The experimenter role advocated here is one which represents the range of sociophenomenological thought from the radical attitude of Husserl's philosophy (Raval, 1972) to the "inquiring man" of personal construct psychology (Bannister & Fransella, 1985). Everything is questioned. This questioning is a questioning out of curiosity and not out of suspiciousness. I make this point before considering in detail the relationship between the experimenter and the subject. If, from our personal construct psychology perspective on the findings relating to subjects as construing people, we conclude that they are well able to collaborate with experimenters, then we must also have experimenters who are able to collaborate with them.

The clinical testing situation provides an illustration of another psychological situation in which subjects are expected to cooperate, in their own best interests. Yet experimenters or testers do not do so. In fact, they share very little of their motives, in Schütz's (1967) sense, and regard this as "professional" behaviour. A professional can be defined as "someone who takes away from the people knowledge and skills which rightly belong to them" (Heather, 1976, p.116). Experimenters, as well as subjects, can be seen as construers of their own experience and as capable of viewing experience from multiple perspectives. On this basis, the process of consultation has been proposed for inclusion in all clinical evaluations by psychologists (Fischer, 1971). In this process the tester attempts to grasp the testee's perspective of the testing situation. The tester also shares motives and impressions, not only of testee with tester, but tester with testee.

Experimenters are Assumed to be Construing People

In this chapter I have explored some of the implications of viewing experimenters as construing people. We found that, if we accept the arguments about the importance of reflexivity in psychological theories, we have to make this assumption about experimenters. There proved to be considerable evidence that experimenters are active construers. This evidence was available in so-called "experimenter errors," in the motives ascribed to their role, in its manipulativeness, and in the myths which experimenters and researchers were found to perpetuate. Mythmakers are, of course, interpreters. I also explored in some detail the evidence for experimenter expectancy effects, since they represent the most thorough demonstration available that experimenters are trying to make sense of their experiences. The findings with regard to experimenters as reflective knowers are, I believe, of even greater importance. It appears that this crucial capacity of experimenters is rarely, in any systematic way, being put to good use. In fact, experimenters are often prohibited from using their capacities as construing or interpreting people.

Traditional psychological perspectives on these findings -- for example, on experimenter expectancy effects -- were found to contain some welcome suggestions. These included building up a body of knowledge of the effects of so-called "experimenter errors" in samples of experimental situations, providing better training for experimenters and creating a new job role, that of the professional experimenter. Some suggestions, however, revealed that the erroneous and distorting interpretations and assumptions inherent in some of the models of Chapter 2 were being made. For example, I questioned the idea that leaving experimenters blind to the purpose of the experiment achieved the "lack of bias" which was desired, given the experimenters' capacities to develop hypotheses of their own. The suggestion that computers would make less biased data collectors than people was also criticised, since it would reduce our work to a psychology of person-and-machine and not contribute to a science of construing people.

Of the personal construct psychology recommendations which we examined, all support the view that experimenters are interpreters and that their construing capacities can be made better use of in the psychological experiment. They advocate maximising the personal involvement of experimenters in their tasks, and this requires getting as close as they possibly can to the phenomena being studied. They advocate the role of pattern perceiver for experimenters, that is, of eliciting structure in the data. And they advocate that experimenters be good listeners, which involves also questioner and collaborator roles.

Having examined these recommendations, it is now possible to consider some of the implications of the assertion that the science of psychology involves an interaction between construing people.

References

Bannister, D. (1970). Comment on H.J. Eysenck. Explanation and the concept of personality. In R.T. Borger & F. Cioffi (Eds.) Explanation in the behavioural sciences (pp.411-418). Cambridge: Cambridge University Press.

Bannister, D. (1976). Schizophrenia as a public fantasy. British Psychological Society Conference, York.

Bannister, D. & Fransella, F. (1985). Inquiring man. Beckenham: Croom Helm.

Barber, T.X. (1972). Pitfalls in research: Nine investigator and experimenter effects. In R.M.W. Travers (Ed.) Handbook of research in teaching (pp.39-56). Chicago: Rand-McNally.

Barber, T.X. & Silver, M.S. (1968). Fact, fiction, and the experimenter bias effect. Psychological Bulletin, 70, 1-29.

Boch, R.D. (1975). Multivariate statistical methods in behavioural research. N.Y.: McGraw-Hill.

Bogdan, R. & Taylor, S.J. (1975). Introduction to qualitative research methods: A phenomenological approach to the social sciences. New York: Wiley.

Brandt, L.W. (1971). Science, fallacies and ethics. Canadian Psychologist, 12, 231-242.

Bronowski, J. (1951). The common sense of science. Middlesex: Penguin.

Bruyn, S.T. (1966). The human perspective in sociology. Englewood Cliffs, New Jersey: Prentice-Hall.

Clarke, A.M.; Michie, P.T.; Andreasen, A.G.; Viney, L.L. & Rosenthal, R. (1976). Expectancy effects in a psychophysiological experiment. Physiological Psychology, 4, 137-144.

Cordaro, L. & Ison, J.R. (1963). Observer bias in classical conditioning of the planarian. Psychological Reports, 13, 787-789.

Deutscher, M. (1983). Subjecting and objecting: An essay on objectivity. St. Lucia: University of Queensland Press.

Dreyfus, H.L. (Ed.) (1982). Husserl, intentionality and cognitive science. Cambridge, Mass.: Bradford/MIT Press.

Epstein, Y.M.; Suedfield, P. & Silverstein, S.J. (1973). The experimental contract: Subjects' expectations of and reactions to some behaviours of experimenters. American Psychologist, 28, 212-221.

111

Farr, J.L. & Seaver, W.B. (1975). Stress and discomfort in psychological research: Subject perception of experimental procedures. American Psychologist, 30, 770-773.

Fischer, C.T. (1971). The testee as co-evaluator. In A. Giorgi, W.F. Fischer & R. Von Eckartsberg (Eds.) Duquesne Studies in Phenomenological Psychology (pp.385-394). Pittsburgh, Pa.: Duquesne University Press, 1.

Fodor, J.A. (1968). Psychological explanation. New York: Random House.

Giorgi, A. (1975). An application of phenomenological method in psychology. In A. Giorgi, C.T. Fischer and E.L. Murray (Eds.) Duquesne Studies in Phenomenological Psychology. Pittsburgh, Pa.: Duquesne University Press, 2, 82-103.

Guetzkow, H.; Kotler, P. & Schultz, R.L. (1972). Simulation in social and administrative science. Englewood Cliffs, N.J.: Prentice-Hall.

Haley, J. (1963). Strategies of psychotherapy. New York: Grune & Stratton.

Harré, R. (1974). Blueprint for a study of science. In N. Armistead (Ed.) Reconstructing social psychology (pp.60-70). Middlesex: Penguin.

Heather, N. (1976). Radical perspectives in psychology. London: Methuen.

Hudson, L. (1975). Human beings. New York: Anchor.

James, W. (1948). Essays in pragmatism. New York: Hafner.

Jourard, S.M. (1968). Disclosing man to himself. New York: Van Nostrand.

Jourard, S.M. (1971). Self-disclosure. New York: Wiley.

Kelly, G.A. (1969). Humanistic methodology in psychological research. Journal of Humanistic Psychology, 9, 53-65.

Laing, R.D. (1961). Self and others. London: Tavistock.

112

‍‍‍

Laszlo, J.P. & Rosenthal, R. (1971). Subject dogmatism, experimenter status and experimenter expectancy effect. Personality, 1, 11-23.

Lefcourt, H.M. (1976). Locus of control. New York: Wiley.

Lefcourt, H.M. (1981). Research with locus of control. New York: Academic Press.

Levy, L.H. (1967). Awareness, learning, and the beneficient subject as expert witness. Journal of Personality and Social Psychology, 6, 365-370.

McGuigan, F.J. (1963). The experimenter: A neglected stimulus object. Psychological Bulletin, 60, 421-428.

Mead, G.H. (1962). Mind, self and society. Chicago: University of Chicago Press.

Milgram, S. (1963). Behavioural studies of obedience. Journal of Abnormal and Social Psychology, 67, 371-378.

Miller, G.A.; Bregman, A.S. & Norman, D.A. (1965). The computer as a general purpose device for the control of psychological experiments. In R.W. Stacy & B.D. Waxman (Eds.) Computers in biomedical research. New York: Academic Press, 1, 467-490.

Mischel, T. (1964). Personal constructs, rules and the logic of clinical activity. Psychological Review, 71, 180-192.

Moreno, Z. (1969). Practical aspects of psychodrama. Group Psychotherapy, 22, 213-219.

O'Donovan, D. (1968). A phenomenological analysis of the laboratory situation. Review of Existential Psychology and Psychiatry, 8, 141-154.

Orne, M.T. (1969). Demand characteristics and the concept of quasi-controls. In R. Rosenthal and R.L. Rosnow (Eds.) Artifact in behavioural research (pp.143-179). New York: Academic Press.

Perrot, L.A. (1977). Research on research: The human dimension. Journal of Phenomenological Psychology, 7, 148-171.

Phares, E.J. (1976). Locus of control in personality. New Jersey: General Learning Press.

Piaget, J. (1930). The child's conception of physical causality. New York: Harcourt Brace & Co.

Plutchik, R. (1968). Foundations of experimental research. New York: Harper & Row.

Raval, R.K. (1972). An essay on phenomenology. Philosophy and Phenomenological Research, 33, 216-226.

Reif, F. (1961). The competitive world of the pure scientist. Science, 134, 1957-1962.

Roe, A. (1961). The psychology of the scientist. Science, 134, 456-459.

Rogers, C.R. (1968). Some thoughts regarding the current presuppositions of the behavioural sciences. In W.R. Coulson & C.R. Rogers (Eds.) Man and the science of man (pp.80-95). Columbus, Ohio: Merrill.

Rosenhahn, R. (1967). On the social psychology of hypnosis research. In J.E. Gordon (Ed.) Handbook of experimental and clinical hypnosis (pp.35-46). New York: Macmillan.

Rosenthal, R. (1967). Covert communication in the psychological experiment. Psychological Bulletin, 67, 356-367.

Rosenthal, R. (1973). On the social psychology of the self-fulfilling prophecy: Further evidence for Pygmalion effects and their mediating mechanisms. New York: MSS Modular Publications.

Rosenthal, R. (1976). Experimenter effects in behavioural research. New York: Appleton-Century-Crofts.

Rosenthal, R. & Fode, K.L. (1961). The problem of experimenter outcomes-bias. In D.P. Ray (Ed.) Series research in social psychology (pp.22-32). Washington, D.C.: National Institute of Social and Behavioural Science.

Rosenthal, R.; Friedman, C.J.; Johnson, C.A.; Fode, K.L.; Schill, T.R.; White, C.R. & Vikan-Kline, L.L. (1964). Variables affecting experimenter bias in a group situation. Genetic Psychological Monographs, 70, 271-296.

Rosenthal, R. & Jacobson, L. (1968). Pygmalion in the classroom. New York: Holt, Rinehart & Winston.

Rotter, J.B. (1966). Generalised expectancies for internal and external control. Journal of Consulting and Clinical Psychology, 80, (Whole No. 609).

Rychlak, J.F. (1970). The human person in modern psychological science. British Journal of Medical Psychology, 43, 233-240.

Schonke, M. (1975). Psychodrama in school and college. Group Psychotherapy and Psychodrama, 28, 168-179.

Schütz, A. (1953). Common sense and scientific enterprise. Philosophy and Phenomenological Research, 14, 1-38.

Schütz, A. (1967). The phenomenology of the social world. Chicago: Northwestern University Press.

Shotter, J. (1970). Men, the man-makers. In D. Bannister (Ed.) Perspectives in personal construct theory (pp.223-254). London: Academic Press.

Skinner, B.F. (1972). Cumulative record. New York: Appleton-Century-Crofts.

Straus, E.W. (1966). Phenomenological psychology - selected papers. New York: Basic Books.

Sullivan, H.S. (1937). A note on the implications of psychiatry, the study of interpersonal relations, for investigations in social science. American Psychologist, 28, 587-591.

Sullivan, H.S. (1953). Conceptions of modern psychiatry. New York: Norton.

Szasz, T. (1973). Ideology and insanity. London: Calder & Boyars.

Toulmin, S. (1970). Reasons and causes. In R. Borger & F. Cioffi (Eds.) Explanation in the behavioural sciences (pp.127-140). Cambridge: Cambridge University Press.

Viney, L.L. (1972). Reactions to frustration in chronically disabled patients. Journal of Clinical Psychology, 28, 164-165.

Viney, L.L. (1983). The assessment of psychological states. Psychological Bulletin, 94, 542-563.

Webb, W.B. (1961). The choice of the problem. American Psychologist, 16, 223-227.

Williams, D.I. (1977). The social evolution of a fact. Bulletin of the British Psychological Society, 30, 241-243.

Wolfendale, G. (1969). Experimentation by computer: Some preliminary steps. British Journal of Mathematical and Statistical Psychology, 22, 199-215.

CHAPTER 5

SOME INTERPRETATIONS OF THE INTERACTION

BETWEEN SUBJECT AND EXPERIMENTER

Can we assume the science of psychology to be a social discipline?

Is there communication between construing people during our data collections?

What are the role expectations of our subjects and experimenters?

Where is the balance of the power in their relationship? How is it maintained?

Are our collections of data as ethical as they might be?

I have already observed that the work of the psychologist can be considered to consist of a process by which one person gets to know another through mutual orientation. This chapter deals with this process from several viewpoints. First, I shall examine some of the grounds for construing the process as an interpersonal one. Then I shall examine some of the empirical evidence in support of that interpretation. The interpersonal interplay between subject and experimenter and subject and psychologist will then be explored. As in Chapters 3 and 4, I shall examine the perspectives of traditional psychology and personal construct psychology on these findings, with the aim of clarifying some aspects of these interactions. Finally, some of the ethical implications of the various models of data collection will be discussed. Ethical issues are crucial for psychologists whose work as construers is with similarly construing people.

Reasoned Grounds for the Interaction

There are, in effect, two reasoned grounds on which the science of psychology may be said to be a social one. Because, firstly, the subject matter of psychology is the person and because the scientist, too, is a person, psychology may be defined as a process which takes place between people. The relationship between subject and experimenter thus becomes crucial (Stringer & Bannister, 1979). The other related grounds on which this assumption is made refer to the actual collection of psychological data. Because it takes place between construing people and because all such people are interpreters of meaning, data collection involves an interaction or sharing of the construed worlds of the people involved. Such communication should take place between subjects as well as objects (Steele, 1982).

Let us look at the more general of these assumptions first. It is, in fact, directly traceable to the early plans for a phenomenologically orientated psychology (Husserl, 1927). This psychology included not only awareness of self, but of others. Such a science cannot be free of social interaction (Schütz, 1967). All of the so-called social sciences may be described as "objective meaning contexts of subjective meaning contexts" (Schütz, 1967, p.127). They involve individually and privately construed worlds which, by the intersubjective standard of science, are shared to form publicly construed worlds.

While phenomenological approaches focus on the subjective, they must prove themselves in intersubjective situations (Shlien, 1965). Psychologists are asking for an extension of traditional definitions of psychology to include the science of people as they are interpreted by other people (Lyons, 1963). This is not to infer that traditional psychologists are all blind to the social character of their discipline. It has been noted that psychology is unique among the sciences in requiring man to obtain knowledge from man himself (Miller, 1972b).

As to our second reasoned ground, personal construct psychology maintains that the system by which each person makes sense of his or her world is an interpersonal one. It follows that the experimenter and subject who take part in psychological research construe their experiences in social terms. Personal construct psychologists have also stated that, when one person construes the constructs of another, this involves taking up a role in relation to that other person. This may even, in symbolic interactionist terms, involve imagining oneself in the role of another. This is what experimenters are called on to do in relation to subjects, to try to understand their construed worlds.

Psychological data collection is then appropriately viewed as the special province of social psychologists. Their role in relation to psychology may be similar to that of epistemologists in relation to philosophy (Friedman, 1967; Manicas & Secord, 1982).

There are many other ways in which the social nature of psychology can be inferred. When people come together they elicit certain patterns of interpersonal behaviour from each other (Leary, 1957). This suggests that there is likely to be a good deal of dynamic interaction between the two people who comprise the basic data collection unit. This assumption can be seen to be implicit in some of the psychological research reported in the literature. For example, psychologists have written about the experimental "contract" between experimenter and subject (Epstein, Suedfield & Silverstein, 1973). They were referring to the expectations each might have of the other and how they might be fulfilled. The term "contract" implied an interactive relationship in the experimental situation, one which must be, moreover, between two construing people. A contract between two nonconstruing people, or even between a construing person and a nonconstruing person, could not be binding.

So much for indirect inference from reported psychological research. Let us now turn to some data which bear directly upon the assumption that the relationship between subject and experimenter is one of social interaction. That I have chosen to assume this to be so is apparent in the Mutual Orientation Model of data collection which I proposed in Chapter 2. Assumptions are not testable interpretations like hypotheses, but they can be supported by evidence. In this case, the evidence includes the effects of the presence and absence of the experimenter as well as the interaction of subject and experimenter characteristics and its subsequent effects on the reactions of the subject. The influence of the relationship between subject and experimenter as it develops prior to the experiment on subsequent experimental reactions of the subject is considered, as are the data from attempts to use subject role play as an experimental tool. Research on these topics is far from complete. Many studies remain to be done. One interesting enquiry has taken the form of a study by participant-observers of the microculture of the psychological laboratory (Farr, 1976). The method of participant observation is described in Chapter 7.

Empirical Grounds for the Interaction

The first question which must be answered from the relevant research is whether the presence or absence of the experimenter affects the experimental performance of the subject in any way. If there is no social interaction during data collection, the absence of the experimenter might not make any difference to the data. This does not appear, however, to be the case. The presence or absence of the experimenter seems to be an influential factor. This has been found to be so even with relatively simple subject responses. Responses to an easy eye-hand coordination task have been shown to be faster when the experimenter was present than when he was absent (Carment & Latchford, 1970). Social facilitation of this response -- that is, quicker responding when working with a fellow subject -- was also only apparent when the experimenter was present. Similarly, electromyogram responses were used to measure subjects' responses to a more complex task of not responding to a tone (Musante & Anker, 1972). The presence of the experimenter was found to facilitate the ability of subjects not to respond when their performances were compared with those in an "experimenter absent" condition. It seems that psychologists should routinely report on the nature of the research interaction in which their data were collected.

The social nature of psychological research can also be demonstrated by referring to some of the work which has been reviewed in Chapters 3 and 4 of this book. This work indicates that the characteristics of both subject and experimenter can affect the outcomes of psychological experiments. It is also important to remember that their characteristics have been shown to interact (Johnson, 1976a; 1976b). Levels of experimenter anxiety have differentially affected the verbal learning task performance of anxious and less anxious subjects (Jabara, 1973). Similar findings have occured for the results of clinical evaluations (Masling, 1960). Also, in a standard tone matching task the expectancies of subject and experimenter have interacted additively when the directions of these expectancies coincided (Zoble & Lehman, 1969). This finding is reminiscent of our finding that similarity between subjects' and experimenters' interpretations of their worlds in terms of their perceived locus of control encouraged experimenter expectancy effects (Clarke et al, 1976).

Some of the effects of different types of interpersonal interactions of subject and experimenter before the start of the experiment have also been examined. However, much more exploration is needed. The relationships of academic staff members with their student subjects provide an example. These relationships have had an effect with subjects whose task was to monitor a visual display (Waag, Tyler & Halcomb, 1973). The group of subjects who worked with an experimenter whom they knew, because he was teaching their psychology laboratory course, correctly detected significantly more signals and tended towards significantly fewer perceived false alarms than did the group of subjects who did not know their experimenter. This finding has been replicated with a task that did not involve reward as the monitoring task had done (Rosenkrantz, Jaffey & Van de Riet, 1975). Similar studies have also been carried out with subjects who have been labelled as schizophrenic and hospitalised (Legan, 1973), as well as with children. Young children have been shown to be more responsive to reinforcement from experimenters whom they could construe effectively because they were familiar with them (Roodin & Simpson, 1976). With regard to the conservation processes of Piaget, children have been shown to be more likely to acquire them in a cooperative rather than a noncooperative instructional setting (Riegel, 1975).

There is an older study which has addressed this phenomenon, too (Kanfer & Karas, 1959). The effects of pre-experimental interaction between experimenter and subject were examined in the context of verbal conditioning, an experimental paradigm similar to that of the reinforcement study described in Chapter 2. Four groups of subjects took part. One group had positive feedback during a prior interaction, and the second group, negative feedback. The third interacted with the experimenter but received no relevant feedback, while the fourth had no interaction. The only apparent effect was that the groups with prior interaction conditioned faster than the one having no prior interaction. There was no demonstrated effect relating to the type of interaction which took place. This effect has also been demonstrated with responses to sexual stimuli in an experimental situation (Abramson et al., 1975). The experimenters and subjects interacted formally or informally before the stimulus presentation began. The informally interacting experimenters, when compared with their more formal counterparts, appeared to encourage more generalised physiological arousal. In this condition more of the kinds of responses to sexual stimuli, which they considered were usually inhibited, were found.

The other main indication that psychological data collection is a social process is the growing use of role play by experimenter and subject to elucidate some psychological problems. Role play implies social interaction. It also implies the involvement of at least two people, subject and experimenter, each of whom is a sufficiently active interpreter and reflective knower to be able to understand and imagine and then to act out the roles. Role play was originally suggested as a data collection technique which might avoid the pitfalls induced by deceiving subjects in psychological experiments (Greenberg, 1967; Seeman, 1969; Stricker, Messick & Jackson, 1969). It has also been used to test hypotheses which could not otherwise be tested (Guetzkow et al., 1963). Role play has not been fully accepted by psychologists, either as an alternative to deception (Miller, 1972a; Mixon, 1974) or for testing hypotheses (Freedman, 1969). Its use, however, is still advocated by some psychologists, for example to make possible comparisons of different procedures for obtaining subject consent to various experimental treatments (Bercheid, et al., 1973). More important for our purposes, it can also be used to discover the meanings that experimental situations have for subjects (Orne, 1969). Role play in psychological data collection implies communication between construing people.

The Interpersonal Interplay of the Research Relationship: Subject and Experimenter, Subject and Psychologist

Some situations are routine and therefore easy for the participants in them to handle. As people take and develop roles in less routine situations they make several assumptions. One is that their interpretation of the situation, or the meaning it has for them, is valid. Another is that others share their interpretation of it. People rarely bother to check their interpretations in these situations (McHugh, 1968). However, the situation in which the research relationship develops is not a routine one for either the subject or the experimenter.

It is not possible to review here all the available evidence of the possible interpersonal interplay during a psychological enquiry because it is very complex (Skuja & Sheehan, 1977). I shall limit myself to only three aspects of it. They are the role expectations, the balance of power, and the alienation of subject and experimenter. Role expectations develop because the people involved in the data collection are construers. Role expectations do exist in psychological experiments. The plea from a subject to an experimenter (Jourard, 1968), which I included in Chapter 4, gives something of the detail of the roles as they are construed in a traditional psychological experiment. It is the expectation of both subject and experimenter regarding the experimenter role that the person filling it will attempt to manipulate the behaviour of the subject without giving any explanations. They also expect of the people in the role of the subject that they will accept this manipulation on the part of experimenters without questioning their aims or intentions. This was so in Lucy's experiment with Linus (in Chapter 2). The effects of self-disclosure by both experimenter and subject in breaking down these role expectations has been demonstrated (Jourard, 1971).

This definition of the subject role as precluding the right to question the experimenter or researcher about the experiment is implicit in what psychologists do or do not do rather than in what they say. It is an important factor in the balance of power between experimenter and subject. Subjects who cannot question have little real choice and so can have little power. In symbolic interactionist terms, they have little to say in the definition of the situation in which they and the experimenter meet. The experimental situation is one of social interaction, but the relationship has some of the characteristics of a superior-subordinate one (Schultz, 1969, p.221). The subjects' lack of power has two bases (Kelman, 1972). One is that subjects are often selected to participate in research from a population which is at a disadvantage in the wider social system, for example, students, hospitalised psychiatric patients or incarcerated prisoners. The other is their relative disadvantage in the research situation as "naive" subjects. For both these reasons, subjects come to construe themselves as lacking in power, much as do people who expect an external rather than an internal locus of control.

Does this balance of power between subject and experimenter matter? Yes, because we run the risk of collecting all our psychological data within this one type of relationship instead of tapping the many types of relationships which people are capable of creating. We may, at present, be producing a "subject psychology", by which I mean a science of the subjected person. This is because we present the experimenter to the subjects with certain cues and bolster his or her appearance with props. Several ways of correcting the bias have been recommended. They include involvement of the subject as participator and new training experiences for the experimenter. The reciprocal participation model of experimentation may also be useful (Sardello, 1971). It is described more fully later in this chapter. Suffice it for now to observe that Sardello has noted that experimenters often use their power to limit the interaction between themselves and their subjects. They limit the capacity of the subjects to develop their own roles. He therefore devised a situation in which the subject, too, has some power over the aims of the interaction and its style. In this reciprocal participation the definition of the experimental situation is closer to being shared between experimenter and subject.

In some respects subject and experimenter are much involved in their interaction in traditional psychological research. Subject and psychologist, however, are quite uninvolved, to the point of alienation (Brandt & Brandt, 1974). Psychologists achieve this alienation by transforming meaningful data from subjects into numbers and drawing conclusions about subjects which do not relate back to people. They also write up the results of this research in the distancing third person. Actually, the American Psychological Association advocated doing away with this style of publication a decade ago, commenting that: "if any discipline should appreciate the value of personal communication, it should be psychology" (APA, 1976). Psychologists, if they are not acting as experimenters, can employ experimenters to maintain actual physical distance from the people to be studied. As a result of this, too, subjects have become alienated from the research process. No doubt some of our traditional ways of viewing the subject, especially in the Self-Orientation and Experimenter Orientation Models of Chapter 2, have led to alienated reactions on their part. It is rarely that a research relationship involving a mutual orientation of one person to another, so that the acts of one respond to and influence the acts of the other, is found.

When we, as psychologists, try to come to know another person, we tend to assume that we must work from an alienated viewpoint (Heron, 1970; Salmon, 1979). We have been shown by personal construct psychology and other sociophenomenological approaches that this is not a necessary assumption. What if we experiment with people rather than on them (Bannister & Fransella, 1985)? Several methodologies have been developed in both psychology and sociology to counteract this alienation. There are the various forms of experiential research (Lilly, 1973), in which experimenters serve as their own subjects. There are also the methods which include experimenter and subject as explicitly involved, together, in a relationship. In ethnomethodology (Garfinkel, 1967; Turner, 1974), for example, the observer tries to understand the meaning that the acts of other people have for them as the actors. The validity of interpretation is then decided on by the actors, the subjects, who created that meaning (Psathas, 1968).

Some Traditional Psychological Perspectives

Most, although not all, of the traditional models of psychological research appear to be based on the assumption of distance between experimenter and subject (Danziger, 1985). This may serve to protect the research psychologist as well as the experimenter. It is apparent in the research which is reported as using deception with subjects. Deception introduces methodological problems (Stricker, Messick & Jackson, 1969). It is not chosen by researchers who view the subject as another interpreting person like themselves, because this reflexivity of interpretation makes it very difficult to do so. Deception is, in fact, something of an embarrassment to psychologists. We may have been unduly naive about its effects. Subjects have been shown to behave as if still deceived even after they have themselves verbalised the true purpose of their experiment (Walster, et al., 1967). Apparently the observed behaviour or verbalisation did not necessarily ensure that the debriefing message would become a meaningful part of their construed worlds. Similarly, debriefing after success and failure deception in a memory study like that described in Chapter 2 was not effective (Silverman, Schulman & Wiesenthal, 1970). The subject's construed world may prove to be relatively inaccessible to psychologists who do not reciprocally share their motives with their subjects, as Schütz has suggested.

This lack of mutual orientation is also apparent in the hidden dialogue between experimenter and subject in a traditional psychological experiment. It may result in the experimenter doing an experiment somewhat different from the one which was planned. In it, the experimenter does not tell the subject everything there is to tell about the experiment. The subject, while appearing to follow the experimenter's instruction, is actually hypothesising about the goals of the experiment and looking for support for his or her hypotheses. Had the experimenter recognised subjects to be interpreters, this hidden dialogue would not have taken place. Psychologists frequently use one of two unsuccessful resolutions to this problem (Lyons, 1970). One involves reliance on theory. However, phenomenologically orientated psychologists are opposed to theories which come between the psychologist and his or her phenomena (Kelly, 1955;

Giorgi, 1970). The other resolution consists of an unfortunate emphasis on the partial processes of psychology - -on perception, cognition and learning -- rather than on the study of the whole person.

"No man is alone in his actions: he always bases himself on the meaning established by others" (Luijpen & Koren, 1969, p.149). Some psychologists working within traditional psychology recognise the social interaction which takes place in a psychological experiment, for example, Orne and Rosenthal. Other psychologists have believed, however, that by creating as nearly sterile a situation as possible in the psychological laboratory they could better maintain the controls of the experimental process. Yet research has "revealed social contamination in the laboratory. The subject and the experimenter provide a stimulus for each other, their respective attitudes, feelings and expectations influencing the data that are collected" (Adair, 1973, p.vii). I believe that the data collection relationship is not "contaminated" but accurately reflects the social nature of psychological research.

Worse criticisms have been written of psychological experiments than that they are "contaminated". The subject and the experimenter have been described as "struggling in the experimental arena for adequacy" (Richards, 1970, p.82). Concern for self-esteem and feelings of competency may, of course, obtrude into the collection of data. They need not, surely, lead to such strife. The relationship between psychologist and subject has been described as like that of a hunter with prey. "The psychologist must outwit and secretly influence the subject. The subject may find it to his advantage to comply or he may attempt to defend his (or her) way of life, his independence, and his privacy. In this running battle any new stratagem of the psychologist is likely to evoke an answering stratagem on the part of the subject" (Criswell, 1958, pp.107-108).

At best it can be said that psychologists have tended to develop as impersonal techniques of data collection as possible, in the interests of pseudo-objectivity. The large range of so-called objective tests available in the field of personality is a case in point. This pseudo-objectivity is misleading because interpersonal subjectivity is an integral part of psychology, so it cannot be ignored or refined out of psychological research. The data collected in a relationship in which there is mutual orientation are likely to be very different from those collected as impersonally as possible (DeWaele & Harré, 1976). The latter can only produce categories for interpretation which have been predetermined and do not reflect the current construing of the people involved.

The Personal Construct Perspective

Psychology needs a methodology through which to express its reflexive view of people. This methodology needs to recognise that when experimenter and subject relate to each other, they do so as active construers and reflective knowers. Such a methodology also calls for changes of title for our heroes, the experimenter and the subject. For the "experimenter," the "researcher" seems to me, from the experience-based perspective, to be an apt title, if not yet fully realised in all its potential for anticipatory interpretation and reflection. But what else can we try in place of "subject"? "Responder" is too passively reactive. "Client" is too close to the notion of being helped. I have chosen to label the role, to follow Schütz's (1967) emphasis on mutual orientation, as the "co-researcher."

Certainly the "co-researcher" aptly describes one if not both of the people who communicate with one another, verbally and nonverbally, in the conversational model (Mair, 1970). This type of conversation progresses as follows. The first stage involves formulations, for example, the swapping of private and public self-concepts between researcher and co-researcher. This is something like Jourard's self-disclosure, but it goes on to include confrontations and their consequences. I give you my sketch of you and discuss it with you and vice versa. The grounds of our beliefs must be provided. Some may come from the sketches we have swapped, and more swapping may occur if we wish. This interaction may have consequences for us both in terms of self-evaluation. If it continues over a series of repeated encounters, greater understanding of each others' construct systems should result. This provides a series of interactions, rather than the "one shot deals" of which many data collections consist (Dunlop, 1979). It also provides a psychological procedure closer to an ordinary social relationship in which expectations of repeated interactions are usually held (McCall et al., 1970). The steps which have been described are just one set of many which fit the Mutual Orientation Model of data collection. More work of this kind is currently being carried out in Britain (Reason & Rowan, 1981).

This mode of interaction based on personal construct psychology also represents the direction in which the humanist Jourard's work was moving, especially in its revision of the subject role. He wanted to regard the subject as a collaborator, and encouraged replication of some of the classical experiments of traditional psychology with this Model. Some interesting results have been obtained, for example, in terms of responses to a word association test (Jourard, 1972). However, all such results have not been in support of his proposition that more valid results stem from more humane experimental conditions (Sheehan, 1982).

Other sociophenomenological psychologists are also to be found employing the Mutual Orientation Model. Two people can communicate in a dialogue which is similar to the "I-Thou" dialogue (Buber, 1970). It is a dialogue in which the "thou" is someone who is able to answer questions of the "I," that is, a reflective communicating knower (Strasser, 1967). The psychological enquiry is a game of question and answer played in controlled conditions. The responsibility of the researcher is to ensure that every communication -- question and answer -- is understood. This dialogical procedure is not necessarily a reciprocal one. Neither does it free the co-researcher to the extent that Sardello's (1971) procedure does.

We have seen how Sardello wishes to redress the balance of power in the experimental interaction. Indeed, it is arguable whether the word "experimental" can be used in describing his model because he wants, like other phenomenologists, to reject all a priori hypotheses which he construes as interfering with the research process. Sociophenomenological psychologists do not, however, go so far. In Sardello's dialogue co-researchers are free to make the meaning of the phenomena for them clear to themselves and to their researchers. Researchers are free to make explicit what is going on in the research situation from the point of view of their co-researchers. The dialogues are taped. The psychologist reads them, firstly, reliving the experience, and, secondly, reflecting on them.

Buber's (1970) description of the "I-Thou" relationship has had a much greater influence in continental Europe than in English-speaking countries (Strasser, 1956). In the United States it has, however, produced an interpretation of research which views the ideal interaction between researcher and co-researcher as a kind of love, a prizing (Rogers, 1965). The "I-Thou" relationship has been proposed as a model for science (Maslow, 1966). A distinction between experiential (interpersonally acquired) and observational (acquired as a spectator) knowledge is made. We need the former as well as the latter. All knowledge, however, is "a resultant of a loving or caring relationship between knower and known" (Maslow, 1966, p.108). There have been echoes of this approach in Britain, "Love reveals facts which, without it, remain undisclosed" (Laing, 1976, p.97). Concerned researchers may become involved participants in research. They value both their own self-knowledge and the knowledge of their co-researchers. They may be more open to what transpires and more liable to be affected or changed in relationships with co-researchers. The people involved in both roles are being changed and changing each other during the research (Von Eckartsberg, 1971). There is a truly mutual involvement in this mode of psychological research.

The Ethical Implications of these Perspectives

I shall deal with the ethical implications of traditional research interactions first. These paradigms use little of the range of inter-relating dynamics available to them. They create a multitude of ethical problems for the psychologist through their undervaluing of the people they study and their preference for certain data collection models. Ethical problems also stem from their lack of reflexivity. On this last point, psychologists could more readily find solutions to ethical problems, such as confidentiality, if they could take a leaf from Tolman's book and say, "If I were a subject...."

There are, in fact, certain rights which subjects give up when they agree to participate in a psychological enquiry. Their privacy may be invaded. They have to donate their personal resources of time and attention. They must surrender their autonomy. They may be exposed to psychologically or physically painful procedures. Finally, they may be at risk of emotional or physical injury (Wolfensberger, 1967). So they put at risk their self-esteem, dignity, comfort, safety, and privacy (Sassoon & Nelson, 1969). I am beginning to wonder why? It seems unlikely that they would do so if they were experiencing themselves as free choosers. Motives such as pleasing the experimenter, not to mention satisfactorily completing a course, must be very powerful.

The hidden rather than open dialogue between experimenter and subject, the generally poor quality of their relationship, and the current view of it as "socially contaminated" and suffering from "subject error" and "experimenter bias" -- all of these contribute to the ethical problems of traditional psychology. Hidden dialogues cannot be openly commented on, so that subjects often have to deal with conflicting information. Luckily, the resulting bind is not long lasting. Subjects can escape the data collection relationship, though probably not without some loss of self-esteem. The poor quality of this relationship means that experimenters are not in touch with subjects' feelings as they should be in a responsible psychological enquiry. The condemnatory view of psychologists of the attempts by both subject and experimenter to act like construing people is also likely to undermine their confidence and limit their range of action. Serving in a traditional psychological experiment can be a noxious rather than a nourishing experience (Perls, 1972). Its manipulations can violate the humanity of the subject (Kelman, 1968).

The lack of power of the subject and the alienation of both psychologist and experimenter from the subject have meant that some form of artificial protection for the subject has been necessary. Codes of ethical behaviour for experimenters have been drawn up (for example, American Psychological Association, 1972; Australian Psychological Society, 1970). British psychologists have been slower to agree on the need for such a set of requirements (British Psychological Society, 1978; 1983). One reason for this might be that they would like eventually to see an empirically based set of laws (Gergen, 1973). Deception would then be prohibited. This would be, not because of the effect it has on the quality of the relationship between experimenter and subject, but because it has been demonstrated to introduce extra sources of error into the data collection (Stricker, Messick & Jackson, 1969; Silverman, Schulman & Wiesenthal, 1970; Baumrind, 1985). Another reason for the delay in Britain might be one which gives me some pause for thought. Choosing an agreed set of values which would be accepted by all psychologists might be difficult, given the different interpretations we may make of our worlds. The British have also shown concern over the lack of consultation with subjects when ethical issues are being examined (Aitkenhead & Dordoy, 1983). Of course, more consultation with representatives of subjects is now taking place through the lay members of ethics committees which are now being set up by research institutions in most Western countries.

All of the data collection procedures which have been proposed appear to be directed towards a psychology of the co-researcher. With such an approach, several of the ethical problems which have been outlined are no longer troubling. To take just two instances, deception is no longer possible if subjects have become co-researchers. Their contribution to achieving the aims of the research become valued. Confidentiality, also, is no longer an issue but an integral part of the relationship between researcher and co-researcher. Incidentally, some traditional psychologists do make use of this approach. It is ironic that they trust it most when they are dealing with reactions of co-researchers which are involuntary, that is, not under their control.

Personal construct psychologists do not, as a rule, have much to say directly about ethics. Their emphasis on individual subjectivity is no doubt the reason. A phenomenologist who shares this emphasis has, however, made some relevant comments (Luijpen, 1963). He maintains that to be an interpreting, reflective knower is to be free. To be thus free to contemplate my being leaves me free to be ethical. The subject, then, who is not free, cannot be ethical. The co-researcher, who is, can. This freedom is apparent in the co-researcher of Mair's conversational model, Strasser's question and answer interview, Sardello's reciprocal interaction and Maslow's loving dialogue. In some of these data collection methods there is freedom to swap roles reciprocally. In others there is freedom for all of the people involved to change. All of them have people communicating with each other in a cooperative relationship and with a common goal. The psychology to which they contribute is an ethical psychology. These models of data collection, it is apparent, require no artificial guarding of the rights of the co-researchers nor an artificial creation of rapport between them and the experimenters, now called the researchers. They share all their results, as in the clinical assessment paradigm (Fischer, 1976). They share not just results but the meanings of their construed worlds. They should also not require any artificial motivation of the co-researchers because their curiosity, an interest in extending the range of their constructs, may be sufficient since it can now be fully satisfied. Similarly, because there is more respect for the co-researcher from the researcher, that researcher is likely to be more genuine, warmer and more empathic than is possible in more traditional psychological research. It seems that the conditions of at least some research should approximate those which have been shown to create an effective helping relationship (Rogers, 1957; Carkhuff, 1969). For ethical reasons as well as practical ones, reports of psychological research should include accounts of the research interaction in which the data were collected.

The Research Interaction is Assumed

This chapter has examined some of the interpersonal interactions involved in the collection of psychological data. We have seen that these interactions may be inferred on logical grounds and from within a sociophenomenological perspective. We have also seen that there is empirical evidence available which points to the occurrence of the interactions. This evidence includes the effects of the experimenter's absence, of experimenter and subject characteristics interacting, of relationships between experimenters and subjects before the enquiry begins, and of different types of interactions between experimenter and subject. All of these aspects of the experimental interaction were observed to alter the subsequent collection of psychological data in some way.

Some of the interplay within the research relationship was then discussed. This included the role expectations for both the roles involved and the power balance, or lack of it, in the experimental situation. The experimenter is the one who appears to have the most say in defining the experimental situation. The subject's capacities for action are quite severely limited. It was also suggested that alienation is a feature of the relationship between both psychologist and experimenter and the subject. Psychologists and experimenters are alienated from their focus of interest in the person of the subject, and, probably as a consequence, the subject is alienated from the research.

More specific models of data collection were then examined. The traditional psychological models were found to include the hidden dialogue of experimenter and subject, deception, and the experiment as socially contaminated. The often poor quality of the interaction between subject and experimenter was noted. The experience-based data collections were found to be in contrast with those more often used in the last respect, because they are based on interaction between construing people. Indeed, they encouraged me to relabel "subjects" for their new role as "co-researchers." This more cooperative role is advocated by phenomenologically oriented psychologists, in fact, for "experimenters" as well. I have relabelled them as "researchers." In the more open dialogues provided by these procedures, they can expect to be changed by the enquiry as the co-researchers may be.

140

The ethical implications of the traditional models were then examined. In such situations subjects were found to have given up some of their personal rights and entered into what appeared to be fairly noxious experiences. To protect subjects who have little real power, arbitrary codes of ethics have been drawn up for psychologists. The personal construct and other phenomenologically oriented models do not seem to necessitate such an externally imposed code, because they require an inbuilt ethical stance of researchers in relation to co-researchers.

These are some of the implications of interpreting the collection of psychological data as a social process between construing people. Much of this social process has still to be explored. This multiperspective view of it has served chiefly to highlight its complexity. I have also taken the opportunity to advocate that psychologists report on the nature of the research relationship in which the data have been collected. I shall now turn my attention to some suggestions for data collection tools for a science of construing people, suggestions which I hope will be of use to psychologists with many differing construct systems.

References

Abramson, P.R. et al. (1975). Experimenter effects of responses to explicitly sexual stimuli. Journal of Research in Personality, 9, 136-146.

Adair, J.G. (1973). The human subject: The social psychology of the psychological experiment. Boston: Little, Brown.

Aitkenhead, M. & Dordoy, S. (1983). Research on the ethics of research. Bulletin of the British Psychological Society, 36, 315-318.

141

American Psychological Association. (1972). Ethical principles in the conduct of research with human participants. Washington, D.C.: APA.

Australian Psychological Society. (1970). Code of Professional Conduct. Australian Psychologist, 5, 77-95.

American Psychological Association. (1974). Publication Manual. Washington, D.C.: APA.

British Psychological Society. (1978). Ethical principles for research with human subjects. Bulletin of the British Psychological Society, 31, 48-55.

British Psychological Society. (1983). Guidelines for a code of conduct for psychologists. Bulletin of the British Psychological Society, 36, 242-244.

Bannister, D. & Fransella, F. (1985). 3rd edition. Inquiring man. Beckenham: Croom Helm.

Baumrind, D. (1985). Research using intentional deception: Ethical issues revisited. American Psychologist, 40, 165-174.

Bercheid, E.; Baron, R.S.; Dermer, M. & Libman, M. (1973). Anticipating informed consent: An empirical approach. American Psychologist, 28, 913-925.

Brandt, L.W. & Brandt, E.P. (1974). The alienated psychologist. Journal of Phenomenological Psychology, 5, 41-52.

Buber, M. (1970). I and thou. Translated by W. Kaufman. New York: Scribner.

Carkhuff, R.R. (1969). Helping and human relations. New York: Holt, Rinehart & Winston.

Carment, D.W. & Latchford, M. (1970). Rate of simple motor responding as a function of coaction, sex of the participants, and the presence or absence of the experimenter. Psychonomic Science, 20, 253-254.

142

Clarke, A.M.; Michie, P.T.; Andreason, A.G.; Viney, L.L. & Rosenthal, R. (1976). Expectancy effects in a psychophysiological experiment. Physiological Psychology, 4, 137-144.

Criswell, J.H. (1958). The psychologist as perceiver, In R. Tagiuri & L. Petrullo (Eds.) Person perception and interpersonal behaviour. (pp. 36-44). Stanford: Stanford University Press.

Danziger, K. (1985). The origins of the psychological experiment as a social institution. American Psychologist, 40, 133-140.

De Waele, J.P. & Harré, R. (1976). The personality of individuals. In R. Harré (Ed.) Personality. (pp. 189-246). Totowa, New Jersey: Rowman & Littlefield.

Dunlop, R. (1979). Experience of ageing: A phenomenological study. Unpublished thesis: Macquarie University.

Epstein, Y.M.; Suedfield, P. & Silverstein, S.J. (1973). The experimental contract: Subjects' expectations of and reactions to some behaviours of experimenters. American Psychologist, 28, 212-221.

Farr, R.M. (1976). Experimentation: A social psychological perspective. British Journal of Social and Clinical Psychology, 15, 225-238.

Fischer, C.T. (1976). The meaning of phenomenological psychology. A.P.A. Division of Philosophical Psychology Newsletter, Spring.

Freedman, J.L. (1969). Role playing: Psychology by consensus. Journal of Personality and Social Psychology, 13, 107-114.

Friedman, N. (1967). The social nature of psychological research. New York: Prentice-Hall.

Garfinkel, H. (1967). Studies in ethnomethodology. New York: Prentice-Hall.

Gergen, K.J. (1973). The codification of research ethics. American Psychologist, 218, 907-912.

Giorgi, A. (1970). Psychology as a human science: A phenomenologically-based approach. New York: Harper & Row.

Greenberg, M.S. (1967). Role playing: An alternative to deception. Journal of Personality and Social Psychology, 7, 152-157.

Guetzkow, H.; Alger, C.F.; Brody, R.A.; Noel, R.C. & Snyder, R.C. (1963). Simulation in international relations. Englewood Cliffs, N.J.: Prentice-Hall.

Heron, J. (1970). The phenomenology of social encounter: The gaze. Philosophy and Phenomenological Research, 31, 243-264.

Husserl, E. (1927). Phenomenology. Encyclopaedia Britannica, 14,17, 699-702.

Jabara, R.F. (1973). The effect of high and low anxious experimenter behaviour on the performance of high and low anxious subjects in a complex verbal learning task. Dissertation Abstracts International, 34 (21-B), 895.

Johnson, R.F.Q. (1976a). The experimenter attributes effect: A methodological analysis. Psychological Record, 26, 67-78.

Johnson, R.F.Q. (1976b). Pitfalls in research: The interviews as an illustrative model. Psychological Reports, 38, 3-17.

Jourard, S.M. (1968). Disclosing man to himself. New York: Van Nostrand.

Jourard, S.M. (1971). Self-disclosure. New York: Wiley.

Jourard, S.M. (1972). Experimenter-subject dialogue: A paradigm for a humanistic science of psychology. In A.G. Miller (Ed.) The social

144

psychology of psychological research (pp. 21-32). New York: Free

Press.

Kanfer, R.H. & Karas, S.C. (1959). Prior experimenter-subject interaction and

verbal conditioning. Psychological Reports, 5, 345-353.

Kelly, G.A. (1955). The psychology of personal constructs. New York: Norton.

Kelly, G.A. (1969). Humanistic methodology in psychological research. Journal

of Humanistic Psychology, 9, 532-565.

Kelman, H.C. (1968). A time to speak. San Francisco: Jossey-Bass.

Kelman, H.C. (1972). The rights of the subject in social research: An analysis in

terms of relative power and legitimacy. American Psychologist, 27,

989-1016.

Laing, R.D. (1976). The facts of life. London: Allen & Unwin.

Leary, T. (1957). Interpersonal diagnosis of personality. New York: Ronald.

Legan, D.R. (1973). Differential effects of pre-experimental patient-experimenter

interpersonal relationships on the reinforced reaction time performance of

process-schizophrenics. Dissertation Abstracts International, 34 (5-A),

2223-2224.

Lilly, J.C. (1973). The centre of the cyclone. New York: Paladin.

Luijpen, W.A. (1963). Existential phenomenology. Pittsburgh, Pa.: Duquesne

University Press.

Luijpen, W.A. & Koren, H.J. (1969). A first introduction to existential

phenomenology. Pittsburgh, Pa.: Duquesne University Press.

Lyons, J. (1963). Psychology and the measure of man: A phenomenological

approach. London: Collier-Macmillan.

Lyons, J. (1970). The hidden dialogue in experimental research. Journal of

Phenomenological Psychology, 1, 19-29.

McCall, G.J.; McCall, M.M.; Denzin, N.K.; Suttles, G.D. & Kurth, S.D. (1970).

Social relationships. Chicago: Aldine.

McHugh, P. (1968). Defining the situation. Indianapolis, Ind.: Bobbs-Merrill.

Mair, J.M.M. (1970). Experimenting with individuals. British Journal of Medical

Psychology, 43, 245-256.

Manicas, P.T. & Secord, P.F. (1982). Implications for psychology from the new

philosophy of science. American Psychologist, 38, 399-414.

Masling, J. (1960). The influence of situational and interpersonal variables in

projective testing. Psychological Bulletin, 57, 65-85.

Maslow, A.H. (1966). The psychology of science. New York: Harper & Row.

Miller, A.G. (1972a) Role playing: An alternative to deception? A review of the

evidence. American Psychologist, 27, 623-636.

Miller, A.G. (Ed.) (1972b). The social psychology of psychological research.

New York: Free Press.

Mixon, D. (1974). If you won't deceive, what can you do? In N. Armistead (Ed.)

(pp. 108-116). Reconstructing social psychology. Middlesex: Penguin.

Musante, G. & Anker, J.M. (1972). E's presence: Effect on S's performance.

Psychological Reports, 30, 903-904.

Orne, M.T. (1969). Demand characteristics and the concept of quasi-controls. In

R. Rosenthal and R.L. Rosnow (Eds.) Artifact in behavioural research.

(pp. 143-179). New York: Academic Press.

Perls, F.S. (1972). In and out of the garbage pail. New York: Bantam.

146

Psathas, G. (1972). Ethnomethodology and phenomenology. Social Research, 3, 35-53.

Reason, P. & Rowan, J. (1981). Issues of validity in new paradigm research. In P. Reason & J. Rowan (Eds.) Human inquiry (pp.127-138). Chichester: Wiley.

Richards, A.C. (1970). Humanistic perspectives on adequate and artificial research. Interpersonal Development, 1, 77-86.

Riegel, K.F. (1975). Subject-object alienation in psychological experiments and testing. Human Development, 1, 77-86.

Rogers, C.R. (1957). The necessary and sufficient conditions of therapeutic personality change. Journal of Consulting Psychology, 21, 95-103.

Rogers, C.R. (1965). Some thoughts regarding the current philosophy of the behavioural sciences. Journal of Humanistic Psychology, 5, 182-194.

Roodin, P.A. & Simpson, W.E. (1976). Behaviour, experience and expression: The phenomenon of nostalgia. APA Convention, Chicago.

Rosenkrantz, A.L.; Jaffey, H. & Van de Riet, V. (1975). The influence of experimenter prior contact on college student performance. Journal of Social Psychology, 95, 283-284.

Salmon, P. (1979). Children as social beings. In P. Stringer & D. Bannister (Eds.) Constructs of sociality and individuality (pp.8-16). London: Academic Press.

Sardello, R.J. (1971). A reciprocal participation model of experimentation. In A. Giorgi, W.F. Fischer & R. Von Eckartsberg (Eds.) Duquesne Studies in Phenomenological Psychology. Pittsburgh, Pa.: Duquesne University

147

Press, No. 1, 58-65.

Press, No. 1, 58-65.

Sassoon, R. & Nelson, T.M. (1969). The human experimental subject in context. Canadian Psychologist, 10, 409-457.

Schultz, D.P. (1969). The human subject in psychological research. Psychological Bulletin, 72, 214-228.

Schütz, A. (1967). The phenomenology of the social world. Chicago: Northwestern University Press.

Seeman, J. (1969). Deception in psychological research. American Psychologist, 10, 409-437.

Sheehan, P.W. (1982). Contrasting research methodologies - humanism vs. standard method. Australian Journal of Psychology, 34, 239-247.

Shlien, J.M. (1965). Phenomenology and personality. In J.M. Wepman & R.W. Heine (Eds.) Concepts of personality (pp.291-332). London: Academic Press.

Silverman, I.; Schulman, A.D. & Wiesenthal, D.L. (1970). Effects of deceiving and debriefing psychological subjects on performance in later experiments. Journal of Personality and Social Psychology, 14, 203-212.

Skuja, E. & Sheehan, P.W. (1977). The human subject: A study of individual experimental participation. Human Relations, 30, 143-154.

Steele, R.S. (1982). Freud and Laing. London: Routledge & Kegan Paul.

Strasser, S. (1956). Phenomenological trends in European psychology. Philosophy and Phenomenological Research, 18, 18-34.

Strasser, S. (1967). Phenomenologies and psychologies. In N. Lawrence & D. O'Connor (Eds.) Readings in existential phenomenology (pp.331-351).

Englewood Cliffs, New Jersey: Prentice-Hall.

Stricker, L.J.M.; Messick, S. & Jackson, D. (1969). Evaluating deception in psychological research. Psychological Bulletin, 71, 343-351.

Stringer, P. & Bannister, D. (Eds.) (1979). Constructs of sociality and individuality. London: Academic Press.

Turner, R. (Ed.) (1974). Ethnomethodology. London: Penguin.

Von Eckartsberg, R. (1971). On experimental methodology. In A. Giorgi, W.F. Fischer & R. Von Eckartsberg (Eds.) Duquesne Studies in Phenomenological Psychology. Pittsburgh, Pa.: Duquesne University Press, No. 1, 66-79.

Waag, W.L.; Tyler, D.M. & Halcomb, C.G. (1973). Experimenter effects in monitoring performance. Bulletin of the Psychonomic Society, 1, 387-388.

Walster, E.; Berscheid, E.; Abrams, D. & Aronson, E. (1967). Effectiveness of debriefing following deception experiments. Journal of Personality and Social Psychology, 6, 371-380.

Wolfensberger, W. (1967). Ethical issues in research with human subjects. Science, 155, 47-51.

Zoble, E.J. & Lehman, R.S. (1969). Interaction of subject and experimenter expectancy effects in a tone length discrimination task. Behavioural Science, 14, 357-363.

CHAPTER 6

TOOLS FOR THE COLLECTION OF DATA

FROM CONSTRUING PEOPLE

Are tools for the collection of data from co-researchers by researchers available
   to us?

Can some existing tools be modified for this purpose?

Are the traditional standards of reliability appropriate for these tools?

Are the traditional standards of validity appropriate for them?

Are all the tools developed from sociophenomenological approaches fit for
   researchers and co-researchers to use?

151

I have shown that interaction can take place between co-researcher (subject) and researcher (experimenter).It is now appropriate to consider whether any tools for data collection are available which make use of their separate capacities to interpret and reflect, and to communicate to each other the results of that reflection. There is no need for any reader, depressed by the criticisms of traditional psychology which have been made so far, to give up the discipline in despair because no satisfactory tools for the collection of experience-based data can be found. Some tools for tapping into the experience of construing people have already been mentioned. I will examine them further in this chapter. Also, other tools which are currently in use (Filstead, 1981) may be expanded to meet the requirements of the Mutual Orientation Model of data collection, the most appropriate for our purpose of the four models defined in Chapter 2.

The discussions in this chapter are based on the assumption that it is possible for one person to tap into the inner world of another. Indeed, as ourselves construing people, psychologists have advantages over biologists and physicists when approaching our subject matter. We have acquired a set of special constructs for understanding people (Peters, 1974) and our relationships with them (Hamlyn, 1974). Schütz has shown how such understanding can be established.

> "I can constantly check my interpretations of what is going on in other people's minds, due to the fact that in the live relationship I share a common environment with them... I can ask you not only about the interpretive schemes you are applying to our common environment. I can also ask you about how you are interpreting your lived experiences, and, in the process, I can correct, expand and enrich my own understanding of you. This becoming aware of the correctness or incorrectness of any understanding of you is a higher level of the We-experience".

(Schütz, 1972, p.171)

Some mutual understanding of the context of an other-directed relationship has been regarded by Richardson (1984) as a validational criterion for the collection of experience-based data. This criterion is the best guarantee against the possibility that co-researchers may be lying. Other important criteria which I have discussed earlier in this volume are the needs for researchers to be aware of their own interpretations and assumptions and for them to provide data which are publicly verifiable.

To argue that data collected using the Mutual Orientation Model is likely to be the best for a psychology which embraces human experience is one thing; to find data collection tools which make this possible is another. If psychologists want to know how people are interpreting events, they should ask them (Kelly, 1955). Many researchers are, however, doubtful about the quality of the subsequent reports of co-researchers. These reports may be incomplete or misleading for a variety of reasons besides lying (Nisbett & Wilson, 1977). Co-researchers may have little awareness of some of their own behaviour, for example, what they have just said or changes in their physiological functioning. They may be unaware of the effects of some events on their own behaviour, such as changes in light illumination causing changes in their pupil dilation. They may also be unaware of the wide range of "unconscious" causative factors proposed by psychoanalysts (Bhaskar, 1982). Often co-researchers also seem unaware of the cognitive processes with which they respond to such events. There are difficulties, then, in such data collection. Yet the assumption that total, accurate recall by co-researchers is possible does not have to be made before they can be considered worthy of consultation. Their responses will not contain references to events of which they are unaware. So long as psychologists who wish to work with experience as well as behaviour recognise this constraint on their findings, such data collection may proceed (Ericsson & Simon, 1984). Many forms of psychological research are only partially successful. Yet they are viable as long as their inherent limitations of content and generalisability are made explicit (Fiske, 1978).

The Mutual Orientation Model of data collection avoids most of the questionable assumptions which reduce the viability of the Self Orientation, Experimenter Orientation, and Reactive Orientation Models. The Mutual Orientation Model may also be ethically more acceptable to many psychologists. It achieves this goal through a communication process that has five stages. At the first stage the researcher makes a request of the co-researcher. At the second, the co-researcher responds. At the third, the researcher reflects on the response of the co-researcher. At the fourth, the researcher reveals the results of that reflection to the co-researcher. At the fifth, the co-researcher confirms or denies that reflection. This model is rarely being used in current research in psychology. In the survey of twenty journals which specialise in reports of psychological research during the years 1982 and 1983, to which I referred earlier, no data collection based on this model was identified. Some psychological researchers, it seems, have come to recognise the experience of construing people as appropriate content for their research. But none in this survey had accordingly adjusted their methods of data collection. Even the Role Construct Repertory Technique which originally emerged from personal construct psychology in a form which met the requirements of the Mutual Orientation Model

154

is now being used in a pseudo-objective way. Researchers who employ it are tending either to deceive their co-researchers or to maintain an impersonal distance in place of the "we-relationship."

In this chapter I shall identify a number of existing data collection tools which meet the requirements of the Mutual Orientation Model. I shall then consider the standards of reliability and validity which are appropriate for such tools. Using my somewhat revised standards, I shall provide a detailed review of the Role Construct Repertory Technique. This tool will be considered at some length because it was originally designed within a sociophenomenological perspective but has been modified in accordance with other more positivist traditions in psychology. It serves as an example by which I can clarify the characteristics of tools that are appropriate for the collection of data from and by construing people.

Existing Data Collection Tools

Many existing data collection tools are not suitable for enabling the researcher to gain access to the experience of the co-researcher. The psychological test, which Anastasi (1982, p.22) has defined as "an objective and standardized measure of a sample of behaviour," is not. The personal construct approach of this volume is concerned with the subjective as well as the objective, meaning as well as measurement, and experience as well as behaviour. Some other tools, however, show more promise. Many of them complete at least the first three stages of the Mutual Orientation Model of data collection in their quest to understand the inner world of another person. Those which do so with an emphasis on the first stage, that is, putting most effort into the preparation of the best requests for the researcher to make of the co-researcher, include personality inventories, self-rating scales, the focussed interview, Q-sorts, the critical incidents method and the Semantic Differential Technique. Those which put their emphasis on the second stage of the co-researcher's response include free association techniques, self-characterisations and self-observations of behaviour. Those which emphasize the third stage of the researchers' reflections on the response from the co-researcher include many of the techniques of attribution theory research, projective techniques and content analysis of the responses of co-researchers. These tools will be described and evaluated, together with some of the sociophenomenological tools which have achieved those last two stages of the researcher revealing the results of his or her reflections to the co-researcher and the co-researcher confirming or disconfirming them.

As I have said, when a personality inventory is used the main focus is on the preparation of the questions for the co-researcher by the researcher. Content validity, that is, the extent to which the questions represent effectively the content of the appropriate pool of items, is sometimes considered important. However, usually the judgement of their representativeness is made by the researcher rather than the co-researcher. More often, empirical criterion keying is used. That is, items are selected according to some external criterion. The responses of the co-researchers are then scored in terms of empirically established behavioural correlates. The Minnesota Multiphasic Personality Inventory is probably the best known example of criterion keying (Dahlstrom, Welsh & Dahlstrom, 1972). However, this inventory has items which tap into the experience of the co-researchers. It could meet the requirements of the Mutual Orientation Model if the fourth and fifth stages of communication between co-researcher and researcher were completed. It should be possible in a clinical situation to do so by consulting with the client as a co-assessor (Fischer, 1985). It should be equally possible to follow the same consultative procedures with the co-researcher when the data collection is for research purposes. The same can be said of self-rating scales.

This is also the case for the focussed interview method. Here the emphasis is also on the first stage of the Model, in which the preparation of the interview schedule is all-important. Such an interview schedule is often nondirective in its style, but its aim is to obtain specific, detailed information while covering the range of relevant content and the depth of feelings associated with it (Merton, Fiske & Kendall, 1956). Its goals are more appropriate to the Mutual Orientation Model than are those of inventories and rating scales. So, too, are its greater flexibility and the closer relationship between researcher and co-researcher which it allows. Indeed, in such an interview, researchers are able to help co-researchers to talk about their experience and relieve them of related anxieties. They can give approval to indicate when co-researchers are responding as requested and even direct their attention to aspects of their experience which they have not reported. In many such interviews the fourth and fifth stages of the Model may be being taken. If not, ensuring that they are should be possible.

The critical incidents method (Flanagan, 1954) also shows such possibilities. Here the emphasis is on the first stage because of the need to clarify the experiential phenomenon for which incidents are to be collected. An example should make this clear. If a psychologist wishes to study the experience of having one's privacy invaded, he or she may do so by asking his or her co-researchers to report, perhaps in a diary, incidents during which they believed this to have occurred. In such work, there is a need to define very clearly the phenomena of interest, in this case privacy and the lack of privacy, before any requests are made to co-researchers. A phenomenological reflection may be the most appropriate way to arrive at these definitions. After the reporting of relevant incidents by the co-researchers and the researchers' reflection on them, the fourth and fifth stages may be completed, as they have been for the phenomenon of privacy (Fischer, 1975).

Since their original development (Stephenson, 1953), Q-sorts have become a popular means of entering the inner world of another. When this tool is used, co-researchers are given a set of cards containing descriptive statements which they are asked to sort into stacks ranging from most to least characteristic of themselves with the highest stacks lying in the middle. This use of a symmetrical, normal distribution makes later application of statistical techniques easier; for example, more robust correlation coefficients can be used. The most work, however, must go into the earlier preparation of the statements by the researcher. The pool of statements is usually related to some psychological theory. For example, a Q-sort has been devised to assess whetherthe co-researchers were making interpretations of themselves and their worlds which were compatible with having mastered the psychological tasks of late adolescence, particularly of having developed a sense of identity (Wessman &

Ricks, 1966). It would have been feasible to continue their data collection by providing their co-researchers with the results of the correlations of their responses and asking for their comments on those results.

The last of the tools which emphasize the first stage of the Model is the Semantic Differential Technique (Osgood, Suci & Tannenbaum, 1957). It was developed to study meaning. Ironically, it is now used for a variety of other purposes, because it provides measurement using a standardised procedure. Co-researchers rate each presented stimulus on a seven-point scale from "good" to "bad," "strong" to "weak," "active" to "passive," and so on. This set of constructs has been shown by empirical studies to be represented by three factors: evaluation, potency, and activity. To complete the fourth and fifth stages of the Mutual Orientation Model, researchers should provide co-researchers with information about their relative use of the evaluation, potency and activity dimensions, and the co-researchers should comment on this feedback.

The next group of tools also are traditionally used to achieve only the first three stages of the model. They focus most on the second stage in which the co-researcher responds to the requests of the researcher. The three examples to be dealt with here are free association techniques, self-characterisation and observations of one's own behaviour. The method of free association has been popular with both Freudian and Jungian analysts, but often with psychotherapeutic goals in view. However, they have been considered by research psychologists (Entwistle, 1968; Cramer, 1968). They have not been much used for this purpose in recent years, perhaps because of difficulties at the third stage of the communication model of data collection. How researchers should interpret the interpretations of their co-researchers when they use this technique is far from clear. If and when this problem is resolved, there is no intrinsic reason why the results of this stage cannot be carried through into the fourth and fifth stage.

Self-characterisation (Kelly, 1955) is the simplest implementation of the assumption that, if researchers want to know about their co-researchers' experiences, they should ask them about them. If the reader asks himself or herself: "Have I anything to say about myself which would be meaningful and useful to a researcher psychologist?", I would guess that the answer will be: "Yes." The instructions for the self-characterisation are as follows:

"I want you to write a character sketch of (name of co-researcher), just as if she were the principal character in a play. Write it as it might be written by a friend who knew her very intimately and very sympathetically, perhaps better than anyone ever could know her. Be sure to write it in the third person."

As for the free association technique, the principal problems with this tool come at the third stage of the Mutual Orientation Model. Although it is useful therapeutically (Fransella, 1980), its future value to psychological research is dependent on the development of ways to deal with the rich data which emerge. Some methods of qualitative analyses are available for such data, but little quantitative analysis has been carried out. A manual for categorising constructs may be useful here (Landfield, 1971). As for the free association technique, the fourth and fifth stage of the Model may then be achieved.

The third technique in this category, observation of one's own behaviour, is similar to the first two in that it was first used in the pursuit of therapeutic goals. This is, of course, the case for many of these psychological tools. It is different in that there are few problems of analysis at the third stage of the Model. Researchers have no difficulty in interpreting their co-researchers' reports because their content has been carefully defined at the first stage. Whether people are reporting on their headaches and the circumstances surrounding them (Mitchell and White, 1977) or their own self-defeating thoughts (Meichenbaum, 1977), the researcher has made clear to them initially the events to which they should attend. For therapeutic purposes, the fourth and fifth stages are often achieved. They should be achieved for research purposes, too.

There are also three tools available for which the first three stages of the Model are apparent, but for which the emphasis is on the third stage. These include techniques used in attribution research, projective techniques, and content analysis of reports from co-researchers. The techniques developed for attribution research have a special place in this survey of tools for tapping into the experiences of the co-researcher, because attribution theory is concerned with understanding the interpretations made by people about other people (Hewstone, 1983). Two techniques have been used for this purpose (Fletcher, 1984). One of these gives little room for the co-researchers' interpretations, but the other provides more. It uses the responses of the co-researchers to open-ended questions which are then interpreted by the researcher. These interpretations may involve the use of statistical analyses like multidimensional scaling (Meyer, 1980; Passer, Kelley & Michela, 1980) or of meaning-based analysis such as content analysis. The latter can, of course, be applied with data from the laboratory (Harvey et al., 1980) or from the field (Harvey, Wells & Alvarez, 1980). Some attribution researchers have gone beyond these first three steps of the Model. Fletcher (1983), for example, obtained co-researcher's attributions from their verbal reports and then had them weigh each attribution in terms of its importance to them as a cause. These tools, too, can be extended to meet the requirements of the Mutual Orientation Model.

The same statement can be made of projective techniques. I have earlier used the Rorschach technique as an example of the preferred model of data collection. When the Rorschach is employed with its full enquiry, it can be seen to follow all of the five stages of the Mutual Orientation Model. The researcher presents the blot, the co-researcher responds to it. The researcher tries to interpret or understand the responses by means of locations and determinants in the blot. He or she tests that understanding with the co-researcher. Finally, the co-researcher confirms or denies the interpretations of the researcher. Such a communication model is likely to be used by psychologists who apply the Rorschach from a phenomenological perspective (Schachtel, 1967). The data interpretation from the results of the enquiry, however, usually moves away from the Model. This is also true for the more structured of the projective techniques, such as those which use pictures in place of blots as the Thematic Apperception Technique does (Bellak, 1970).

The third tool to be considered here is the content analysis of reports from the co-researcher. Content analysis has the advantages of dealing with meaning and encouraging psychologists to use care in defining their interpretation. It is not situation specific but is nonintrusive. It is a method of reflection which can be used for the interpretation of co-researcher responses to projective techniques as well as attribution theory techniques. One use of it has been in combination with simulated situations (Davison, Robins & Johnson, 1983). Co-researchers are presented with tape recordings that simulate interactions in different kinds of situations and are asked to play a role in them. Their performances are taped, together with their responses to requests for introspection on their thoughts which are made at appropriate intervals on the tape. Content analysis is applied to their responses.

For psychological researchers who wish to use statistical techniques, content analysis has the disadvantage of resulting only in categorical scaling. Ordinal scaling is achieved by developing content analysis scales, which make possible a comparison of the experience of one person with another (Viney, 1981). It also provides the opportunity to build up a body of information about the public verifiability of the scores and their validity (Viney, 1983a). The Sociality Scale, for example, was designed to assess the extent to which co-researchers are experiencing themselves to be participating happily in interpersonal interactions (Viney & Westbrook, 1979). The content of the co-researchers' responses that is categorized includes references to solidarity relationships, in which people are construed as resources (e.g., "I can work well with these people"). Intimacy relationships, in which people are construed as sources of personal satisfaction (e.g., "I love Joe"), are also scored. So are influence relationships, in which people are construed as sources of power (e.g., "He told me to be careful"). Frequency scores for the content categories are adjusted according to the length of the scored responses. Evidence of the public verifiability of this method of coming to know another person's inner world is available in the reported agreements between independent scorers.

Comparisons with samples of co-researchers is possible. Evidence of validity has been built up. High scorers on the Sociality Scale have been found to relate more positively to others. They tend to maintain relationships better and to show more interpersonal skills than the low scorers. Reports of the use of such scales can be quantitative (Viney & Westbrook, 1982) or qualitative (Viney, 1983b). But what of the fourth and fifth stages of the Mutual Orientation Model? Can researchers provide feedback for co-researchers in terms of content analysis of their spontaneous reports, and can subjects then confirm or disconfirm it? Refinements of this kind are being investigated (Crooks, 1984).

I have chosen to concentrate in this review of existing data collection tools on those which, while they do not necessarily complete all five stages of the Mutual Orientation Model of data collection, can do so with some minor adjustments. It is appropriate, however, to crovide a reminder of the data collection tools which have been identified elsewhere in this volume as meeting the requirements of the Model by dealing with the last two stages of communication between co-researcher and researcher as well as the first three. They fall into two groups. The first consists of those which have been generated by the phenomenological psychologists at Duquesne University in the United States: for example, reciprocal interaction (Sardello, 1971), the exploratory technique (Collaizi, 1973), consultation with co-researchers (Fischer, 1975), and interactive thematic analysis (Giorgi, 1975). The second group have developed in Britain largely within a personal construct tradition: for example, the conversational model (Mair, 1970) and the search for common constructs in an "I-Thou" relationship (Shepherd, 1982). Use of these tools for data collection is rarely reported in the psychological literature. This may be because it is difficult to determine whether they meet the standards of reliability and validity which have been required of psychological tools (American Psychological Association, 1974).

Reliability and Validity: Some Redefinitions

Reliability has traditionally been defined as the consistency of assessment by the data collection tool, and validity as the extent to which it assesses what it claims to assess. Both constructs have often been defined in statistical terms. Such terms are appropriate, of course, only to tools which measure. Since tools which meet the requirements of the Mutual Orientation Model are as likely to result in qualitative as quantitative assessment, such concepts of reliability and validity may be inappropriate. Standards such as authenticity and attestability may be more appropriate (Brown & Sime, 1981). But are there other aspects of these two sets of standards that are relevant for these data collection tools?

Reliability or consistency of assessment is best considered first. I have already acknowledged the criterion of interpersonal agreement, or public verifiability of private constructs, as relevant to all data collection tools. However, this criterion may not be easy to achieve, since the experience of a co-researcher can only be directly known by that co-researcher (Kendler, 1981). If two independent researchers make the same interpretations of the co-researcher's responses at the third stage of the Mutual Orientation Model, this is a valuable achievement of consistency. Similarly, if the researcher and the co-researcher prove to be in agreement at the last stage of the Model about the researcher's interpretations of those of the co-researcher, that consistency, too, is important.

Consistency of assessment over time may, however, be less appropriate (Mischel, 1968; 1984). The Mutual Orientation Model of data collection has been devised to tap into the ongoing stream of experience of each co-researcher (James, 1890). His or her experience of events is always changing, so that generalisability from one assessment occasion to another is not possible (Gergen, 1973). Nor, when such an assumption is made, is consistency within the assessment instrument on even one occasion, that is, internal consistency, necessarily to be expected. Both researchers and co-researchers should learn from their involvement in data collection, so that the experience of the co-researcher which will be tapped may change from moment to moment. Each tap into the co-researcher's experience is like dipping into a river with a bucket. Just as an ethologist cannot expect to understand the nature of a river from one or even two bucketfuls, a psychologist cannot expect to understand the nature of a co-researcher's total experience from one or two interactions. Psychologists must always expect to limit the generalisability of research findings. When they are dealing with human experience, the limits include the fact that no static picture can be grasped. Social scientists who wish to apply the paradigms of the sciences of the physical world to the sciences of people (Nicholson, 1983) ignore this. Personal construct psychology views traditional reliability as an index of the extent to which a test is insensitive to change (Bannister & Fransella, 1985). For the Mutual Orientation Model, which deals with experience as well as behaviour, reliability may be better conceptualised as dealing with inconsistency rather than consistency, that is, as an index of sensitivity to change.

Some readers may find it difficult to accept this new concept of reliability. If so, at least one other resolution of the consistency problem in the assessment of experience-based constructs is available. The "transition experiment" involves a multiple research design in which the observational techniques used are varied systematically (Campbell, 1957). However, one facet of the design is always identical with the original experiment. No assumption about the replicability of psychological data collections is made. Similarly, a data collection method tapping experience might be incorporated in a multiple approach to data collection, in which aspects of the method would be varied but the total approach would still include the original method. In this way a network of information about the method, much like the nomological network of empirical information to demonstrate the validity of an assessment tool (Cronbach & Meehl, 1955), can be built up.

Validity is more concerned with accuracy than consistency. Three types of validational evidence have been provided for psychological data collection tools so far: content, criterion, and construct validity (American Psychological Association, 1974). Tools which have been effectively designed to collect data from construing people have little need to demonstrate their content validity. These tools, which conform to the Mutual Orientation Model, ensure that the material tapped comes from the co-researcher primarily and from the researcher only secondarily. The relevance of their content to the experiences of the interpreting co-researcher is thus guaranteed. Criterion validity may be established by using either of two types of criteria. One type involves assessing similar experiences in different co-researchers, so that several independent reports come to confirm each other. The other uses a criterion in a realm other than experience, for example, relating mothers' reported experience of childbearing to their mothering behaviour with their infant (Westerink, 1983).

The criteria used for this type of validity may be concurrent or predictive. It is construct validity, however, which seems to be the most important type of validity for these experience-based tools (Wylie, 1979). In this type, it is theory-based predictions, or the interpretations of the researchers, which are compared with the experience-based reports. There can be no completely satisfactory independent criterion to serve in validational comparisons for reports of one person's experience to another. The Mutual Orientation Model, however, ensures that they do arise in the co-researcher's experience and not that of the researcher alone. With that Model, also, honesty is maximized. It therefore seems wisest to collect a range of information about each data collection method, including information related to criterion and construct validity. It is also advisable to pay attention to the relationship between co-researcher and researcher, to ensure maximum accuracy of report. The Mutual Orientation Model provides a mode of communication through which such accuracy is encouraged.

Validity may be viewed as the capacity of a data collection method to tell us what we already know (Kelly, 1955). This comment has been justified by some of the attempts which have been made to demonstrate criterion validity. The criteria for such attempts need to be selected carefully but with considerable imagination. Kelly's personal construct theory has more to contribute to the important construct of validity in data collection, however. His view of people as scientists reminds us that validity is characteristic of interpretations or constructs that allow their creators to anticipate effectively what is going to happen to them. Predictive criterion validity is one form of this notion. It can also be expanded to equate validity with usefulness. If data collection tools for construing people can provide useful as well as accurate information for psychologists, then they are worth developing. They may be said, in that sense at least, to be valid.

The Role Construct Repertory Technique

Since the Role Construct Repertory Technique was developed (Kelly, 1955), it has become one of the tools most frequently used to collect experience-based data (Beail, 1985). It is a personal construct psychology technique that has been referred to frequently in earlier chapters of this book. It seems worthwhile, then, to take some time now to describe the technique, review its usage during the past thirty years and evaluate its reliability and validity.

The Role Construct Repertory Technique requires co-researchers, as I described in Chapter 3, to think of people they know who fit a number of different roles. Bipolar constructs are then elicited by comparing three role fillers at a time: "Think of a way in which two of these people are alike and the third is different from them." A picture of the constructs making up the inner world of a co-researcher results. In an extension of this procedure, a grid matrix is used (Fransella & Bannister, 1977). Role titles are written along the top of the grid and the elicited constructs down the side. Co-researchers place a tick in the grid square if they see the person filling the role in that column as being described by the first pole of each construct. If the subject has described the first two role fillers as "quick" rather than "slow," each role filler must be considered in terms of "quickness." This procedure yields a means of assessing relationships between co-researchers' constructs and their roles. Constructs are sometimes provided by the researcher rather than elicited from the co-researcher. The implications of each construct for other constructs in each person's construct system can be assessed, as can its place in the hierarchy of that system.

It is relatively easy to examine the uses to which the Role Construct Repertory Technique has been put, because the Personal Construct Clearing House, with its loosely related network of international researchers, has provided an annual reading list for its members. A history of personal construct psychology has also been written (Niemeyer, 1983). This history indicates that the technique has been the chief data collection tool used by personal construct psychologists. This review covers the years up to 1980. However, my own review of such research from 1981 to 1983 provides some worrying information. While many forms of the Role Construct Repertory Technique have been in use in psychology so far this decade, they have often been used without proper consideration of the sociophenomenological theory from which it developed. This concern has already been raised (Fransella & Bannister, 1977), but to little effect. It remains a concern because it leads to violations of the Technique as tool for collecting data from and by construing people. Many of the studies in the more recent review were in the area of clinical assessment and very few cast any light on their parent theory. The other large group of studies evaluated scoring methods, statistical analyses, and computer software for use with the Technique. While this group of studies is needed, its preponderence indicates the extent to which measurement has taken precedence over meaning for many Technique users. The other cause for concern in this recent review is that in many cases the original Role Repertory Technique had been whittled down so as to minimize the relationship between co-researcher and researcher, another development alien to the sociophenomenological roots of the Technique.

The reliability of the Role Construct Repertory Technique is still being established. The first type of consistency I see as important, intersubjective agreement, has rarely been examined for the Technique. In its place have stood complex statistical analyses, which are, of course, totally replicable (barring errors). As to consistency over time, there can be no expectation that the results from the use of the Technique on one occasion will be the same as those on another. Using the Technique of itself alters the construct system of the co-researcher and sometimes of the researcher, too. It has even been proposed that an estimate of consistency on the Technique be used, because of the lack of flexibility in co-researchers that it indicates, as a measure of psychopathology (Bannister, 1960). There is considerable evidence to support my alternative construct of reliability, that the Technique sensitively assesses change (Bannister & Fransella, 1985).

The validity of the Technique, like its reliability, will be dealt with in terms of the construct of validity proposed in this chapter. Content validity for it is not in question so long as the constructs are elicited from the co-researchers. When they are provided by the researchers their relevance to the co-researchers should be evaluated. Perhaps psychologists who use this form of the Technique should show independent evidence from their co-researchers that they can understand the provided constructs and use them effectively. As for other data collection tools of this type, there is no independent criterion available for the experiential structures which the Technique reveals. Comparisons with a variety of criteria help, however, to develop a validational network. An experience-based criterion was used to tap the constructs of a client before and after a suicide bid with the Technique and with another means of assessing constructs about dying (Rigdon, 1983). A behaviourally based criterion was used to relate the Technique-established constructs of Australian aboriginals about their households to their behaviour in relation to government supplied housing (Ross, 1983). The ability of the Technique to predict future criteria, that is, predictive validity, has been demonstrated in a Technique-based study of change in a psychotherapy group (reported in Appendix D of Fransella & Bannister, 1977). Demonstrations of construct validity have been more complex. One example is the demonstration that the Technique could be used with stutterers together with psychotherapy. The fact that both derived from personal construct psychology enhanced the meaning of results from the Technique (Fransella, 1982). Finally, considerable evidence of the usefulness of the Technique has been found, for example, in understanding how interpersonal relationships develop (Lea & Duck, 1982), how people learn (Pope & Shaw, 1983), and how addicts choose their drugs of addiction (Leenars, 1981).

While the Role Construct Repertory Technique has gone some way to meet traditional standards of reliability and validity, it may be that in doing so it has moved away from the Mutual Orientation Model of data collection. The increased alienation between co-researcher and researcher that I have reported supports this view, as does the use of provided constructs and heavy reliance on statistical rather than human interpretations of the resulting data. Even when these changes from the original Technique are not made, the Technique achieves only three of the five stages inherent in the Mutual Orientation Model of data collection. The researcher makes a request of the co-researcher, to which the co-researcher responds; then the researcher reflects in some way on that response. The fourth stage, at which the researcher reveals the result of that reflection to the co-researcher, and the fifth stage, in which the co-researcher confirms or denies the reflection, are not achieved. It is a sad commentary on present-day psychology that psychologists often report in private that they have made this important test but rarely are able to do so publically in psychological journals.

Tools for Researchers and Co-researchers

Psychologists are increasingly concerned about interpreting the interpreters. That is, they are wanting to tap into the experiences of co-researchers, using the experiences of researchers. This involves checking to see whether the constructs of the researchers, after data collection, now include the constructs of the co-researchers (Menzel, 1978; Manicas & Secord, 1982). The Mutual Orientation Model of data collection meets this criterion if all of its five stages of communication are achieved. Those data collection techniques that can be used in ways which fit with that Model can be applied to collect data from and by construing people. As new methods develop to fit this model, they will tend, it seems, to focus more on the intentions of the people involved in the data collection and their cognitive processes and language. The results of an increased emphasis on experience may lead to as many verbal as statistical interpretations of the resulting data. It should also lead to a better understanding of behaviour.

In this chapter I have analysed the five stages of the Mutual Orientation Model of data collection and shown how many existing data collection techniques, with minor modifications, may be used in order to know something of the inner world of another person. The sociophenomenological approach which gave rise to the Model has also required a reformulation of the constructs of reliability and validity as they are currently used as criteria for psychological methods. The Role Construct Repertory Technique has been evaluated and found wanting more than would have been expected, given its genesis in personal construct theory. It, like the other data collection tools, can be modified to fulfill sociophenomenological as well as traditional goals (Argyle, 1978). In the final chapter of this book, I shall examine some of the traditional areas of psychological research. I shall try to show how these methods of data collection, or others like them, can be used to build a science of people as interpreters.

References

Anastasi, A. (1982). Psychological testing. New York: Macmillan.

Argyle, M. (1978). Discussion chapter: An appraisal of the new approach to the study of social behaviours. In M. Brenner, P. Marsh & M. Brenner (Eds.) The social context method (pp.237-255). London: Croom Helm.

American Psychological Association. (1974). Standards for educational and psychological tests. Washington, D.C.: APA.

174

Bhaskar, R. (1982). Emergence, explanation and emancipation. In P.F. Secord, (Ed.) Explaining social behaviour. (pp.123-133). Beverly Hills, Calif.: Sage.

Bannister, D. (1960). Conceptual structure in thought disordered schizophrenics. Journal of Mental Science. 106, 1230-1239.

Bannister, D. & Fransella, F. (1985). Inquiring man. Beckenham: Croom Helm.

Beail, N. (Ed.) (1985). Repertory grid technique in personal construct theory. Beckenham: Croom Helm.

Bellak, L. (1970). The TAT and CAT in clinical use. New York: Grune & Stratton.

Brown, J. & Sime, J. (1981). A methodology for accounts. In M. Brenner (Ed.) Social method and social life. London: Academic Press.

Campbell, D.T. (1957). Factors relevant to the validity of experiments in social Psychological Bulletin. 17, 39-44.

Collaizi, P.F. (1973). Reflection and research in psychology: A phenomeno-logical study of learning. Dubuque, Iowa: Kendall Hunt.

Cramer, P. (1968). Word association. New York: Academic Press.

Cronbach, L.J. & Meehl, P.E. (1955). Construct validity in psychological tests. Psychological Bulletin. 52, 281-302.

Crooks, L. (1984). The use of content analysis dimensions and research participants' perceptions of these dimensions. Wollongong: Unpublished paper.

Dahlstrom, W.G.; Welsh, G.S. & Dahlstrom, L.E. (1975). An MMPI handbook. Minneapolis: University of Minnesota Press.

Davison, G.C.; Robins, C. & Johnson, M.K. (1983). Articulated thoughts during simulated situations: Cognitive Therapy & Research. 2, 17-40.

Entwistle, D.R. (1968). Word associations of young children. Baltimore: Johns Hopkins.

Ericsson, K.A. & Simon, H.A. (1984). Protocal analysis: Verbal reports as data. Cambridge, Ma.: MIT Press.

Filstead, W.J. (1981). Using qualitative methods in evaluation research. Evaluation Review. 5, 259-268.

Fischer, C.T. (1975). Privacy as a profile of authentic consciousness. Humanitas 4, 27-43.

Fischer, C.T. (1985). Individualizing psychological assessment. Monterey, California: Brooks/Cole.

Fiske, D.W. (1978). Strategies for personality research. London: Jossey-Bass.

Flanagan, J.C. (1954). The critical incident technique. Psychological Bulletin, 51, 327-338.

Fletcher, G.J.O. (1983). The analysis of verbal explanations for marital separation: Implications for attribution theory. Journal of Applied Social Psychology. 13, 245-258.

Fletcher, G.J.O. (1984). Psychology and common sense. American Psychologist, 39, 203-213.

Fransella, F. (1980). Nature babbling to herself: The self characterisation as a therapeutic tool. In J.G.S. Bonarius & S. Rosenberg (Eds.) Recent advances in the theory and practice of personal construct psychology. (pp.27-39). London: Macmillan.

Fransella, F. (1978). Personal change and reconstruction: Research on a treatment of stuttering. London: Academic Press.

Fransella, F. & Bannister, D. (1977). A manual for the Repertory Grid Technique. London: Academic Press.

Gergen, K.J. (1973). The codification of research ethics. American Psychologist. 28, 907-912.

Giorgi, A. (1975). An application of phenomenological method in psychology. In A. Giorgi, C.T. Fischer & E.L. Murray (Eds.) Duquesne studies in phenomenological psychology. Pittsburgh, Pensylvania: Duquesne University Press, No. 2, 82-103.

Hamlyn, D.W. (1974). Person perception and our understanding of others. In T. Mischel (Ed.) (pp.67-96). Understanding other persons. Oxford: Blackwell.

Harvey, J.H.; Wells, G.I. & Alvarez, M.D. (1980). Attribution in the context of conflict and separation in close relationships. In J.H. Harvey, W. Ickes & R.F. Kidd (Eds.) New directions in attribution research. (pp.235-260). Hillsdale, N.J.: Laurence Erlbaum.

Harvey, J.H.; Yarkin, K.L.; Lightner, J.M. & Town, J.P.O. (1980). Unsolicited interpretation and recall of interpersonal events. Journal of Personality and Social Psychology. 38, 551 - 568.

Hewstone, M. (Ed.) (1983). Attribution theory: Social and functional extensions. Oxford: Blackwell.

James, W. (1890). Principles of psychology. New York: Holt.

Kelly, G.A. (1955). The psychology of personal constructs. New York: Norton.

Kendler, H.H. (1981). Psychology: A science in conflict. New York: Oxford.

Landfield, A.W. (1971). Personal construct systems in psychotherapy. New York: Rand-McNally.

Lea, M. & Duck, S. (1982). A model for the role of similarity of values in friendship development. British Journal of Social Psychology. 21, 301-310.

Leenars, A.A. (1981). Drugs and people: Repertory grid structure and the construal of two different kinds of target. Journal of Clinical Psychology. 37, 198-201.

Mair, J.M.M. (1970). Experimenting with individuals. British Journal of Medical Psychology. 43, 245-256.

Manicas, P.T. & Secord, P.F. (1982). Implications for psychology from the new philosophy of science. American Psychologist. 38, 399-414.

Meichenbaum, D. (1977). Cognitive behaviour modification: An interpretive approach. New York: Plenum.

Menzel, H. (1978). Meaning - Who needs it? In M. Brenner, P. Marsh & M. Brenner (Eds.) The social context of method. (pp.142-156). London: Croom Helm.

Merton, R.E.; Fiske, M. & Kendall, P.L. (1956). The focussed interview. New York: Free Press.

Meyer, J.P. (1980). The causal attribution for success and failure: Investigation of dimensionality, formulation and consequences. Journal of Personality and Social Psychology. 67, 707-718.

Mischel, W. (1968). Personality and assessment. New York: Wiley.

Mischel, W. (1984). Convergences and challenges in the search for consistency. American Psychologist. 39, 351-364.

Mitchell, K.R. & White, R.F. (1977). Behavioural self-management: An application to the study of migraine headaches. Behaviour Therapy. 8, 213-222.

Nicholson, M. (1983). The scientific analysis of social behaviour. London: Pinter.

Niemeyer, R.A. (1983). The development of personal construct psychology. Some sociohistorical objectives. In J. Adams, Webber & J. Mancuso Applications of personal construct theory (pp.155-172). New York: Academic Press.

Nisbett, R.E. & Wilson, T.D. (1977). Telling more than we know: Verbal reports on mental processes. Psychological Review, 84, 231-259.

Osgood, C.E.; Suci, S.J. & Tannenbaum, P.H. (1957). The measurement of meaning. Urbana, Ill.: University of Illinois Press.

Passer, M.W.; Kelley, H.H. & Michela, J.L. (1978). Multidimensional scaling of the causes for negative interpersonal behaviour. Journal of Personality and Social Psychology. 36, 955-962.

Peters, R.S. (1974). Personal understanding and personal relationships. In T. Mischel (Ed.) Understanding other persons. (pp.107-120). Totowa, New Jersey: Rawson & Cuttlefield.

Pope, M.L. & Shaw, M.L.G. (1983). Personal construct psychology in education and learning. International Journal of Man-Machine Studies. 14, 223-232.

Richardson, A. (1984). The experiential dimension of psychology. St. Lucia: Queensland University Press.

Rigdon, M. (1983). Death threat before and after attempted suicide: A clinical investigation. In F. Epting & R.A. Niemeyer (Eds.) Personal meanings of death. (pp.112-122). New York: Hemisphere.

Ross, H. (1983). An alternative to conventional methods of eliciting constructs. In Viney, L.L. (Ed.) Australasian Personal Construct Psychology Conference. Wollongong: University of Wollongong.

Sardello, R.J. (1971). A reciprocal participation model of experimentation. In A. Giorgi, W.F. Fischer & R. Von Eckartsberg (Eds.) Duquesne studies in phenomenology psychology. Pittsburgh, Pa.: Duquesne University Press, No. 1, 58-65.

Schachtel, E.G. (1967). Experiential foundations of Rorschach's test. London: Tavistock.

Schütz, A. (1972). Phenomenology of the social world. London: Heinemann.

Shepherd, E. (1982). Coping with the first person singular. In E. Shepherd & J.P. Watson (Eds.) Personal meanings (pp.33-46). Chichester: Wiley.

Stephenson, W. (1953). The study of behaviour: Q technique and its methodology. Chicago: University of Chicago Press.

Viney, L.L. (1981). Content analysis: A research tool for community psychologists. American Journal of Community Psychology. 9, 269-281.

Viney, L.L. (1983a). The assessment of psychological states through content analysis of verbal communications. Psychological Bulletin. 94, 542-563.

Viney, L.L. (1983b). Images of Illness. Malabar: Krieger.

180

Viney, L.L. & Westbrook, M.T. (1979). Sociality: A content analysis for verbalisations. Social Behaviour and Personality, 7, 129-137.

Viney, L.L. & Westbrook, M.T. (1982). Patterns of anxiety in the chronically ill. British Journal of Medical Psychology, 5, 87-95.

Westerink, J. (1983). Childbirth: Experiences, behaviour and situations. Unpublished doctoral thesis: University of Wollongong.

Wessman, A.E. & Ricks, D.F. (1966). Mood and personality. New York: Holt, Rinehart & Winston.

Wylie, R.C. (1979). The self concept. Nebraska: University of Nebraska Press, Vols. 1 & 2.

CHAPTER 7

TOWARDS A SCIENCE OF CONSTRUING PEOPLE

Can psychologists combine the sociophenomenological approach with more
traditional approaches?

Might meaning become as important to us as measurement?

What criteria for the acceptance or rejection of findings can be used with this
sociophenomenological approach?

To what range of questions can it provide answers?

How can we contribute to a science of construing people?

A theoretical and methodological foundation for a psychology of construing people has now been established. It remains for me to indicate some ways in which psychology can be elaborated, extended, and altered so that it can use tools that are selected because of their relevance to the subject matter of our study. That subject matter, of course, is people. The image of the person that emerges from psychology must be a full image, that is, one taking into account his or her capacities as an actively interpreting being. It follows, too, that the methods suggested should also permit researchers to use their full range of active interpreting in their relationships with their co-researchers.

Psychologists have been asking for new paradigms for some time now. So, too, have other disciplines which provide a theoretical groundwork for the professions concerned with helping people, such as social work (Heineman, 1985; Haworth, 1984; Imre, 1984; Salner, 1984). Yet new paradigms are adopted only slowly and in a step-by-step fashion (Reinharz, 1979). Feyerabend has called for a more flexible approach for science generally, a less rigid adherence to scientific paradigms (Kuhn, 1962). "Science is an essentially anarchistic enterprise: theoretical anarchism is more humanitarian and more likely to encourage progress than its law-and-order alternatives" (Feyerabend, 1975, p.10). This is an extreme position, but one also adopted by the "new paradigm" group in Britain (Reason & Rowan, 1981a). Generally, however, commentators on psychology have been more gentle in their admonitions. Psychology may be attempting to answer too complex a set of questions to permit the use of just one paradigm to find their answers. "More is to be gained by using every kind of scientific approach which pays off" (Scriven, 1969, p.17). Further paradigms may, then, be sought within the constraints of a science of psychology as a careful and disciplined approach to knowledge which is as free from bias as possible.

One of the most important aspects of a paradigm is the data collection model that it promotes. In Chapter 2 four data collection models were explored. They were the Self-Orientation Model, the Experimenter Orientation Model, the Reactive Orientation Model, and the Mutual Orientation Model. Only the last-named model was found to be free of questionable assumptions about the subject and the experimenter, assumptions which have been demonstrated, in Chapters 3 and 4, to be erroneous and misleading. The first two models were also found to evoke some misleading interpretations of the interpersonal interaction of the data collection which have been discussed in Chapter 5. The Mutual Orientation Model, then, in all its five stages, seems the most productive for psychology. My preference for this model of cooperation between researcher and co-researcher for many types of psychological enquiries is again apparent in this chapter. Some of the data collection tools which may achieve the five stages were reviewed, together with some standards for their evaluation, in Chapter 6.

It is personal construct psychology, together with other socio-phenomenological approaches, which I have pursued here as a source of new perspectives on psychological research. Some writers have been wary about combining these approaches with psychology in its present positivist form. Others, however, are hopeful of a fruitful match (Wetherick, 1970; Giorgi, 1975a; Ashworth, 1976; Filstead, 1979). I believe that they may serve as aids to traditional psychology (Farber, 1966). It is in this spirit that the present chapter is written. We must be aware, however, that taking this view involves more than a fuller realisation of our subject matter and of the interpersonal interactions within which we collect our data. We may even come to reflect on our experience without presupposing causes as we know them (Mixon, in press). Psychologists will then be searching for patterns of relationships of different kinds within and among phenomena for which there is some intersubjective agreement (Reason & Rowan, 1981b; Giorgi, Barton & Maes, 1983; Hyland, 1985).

This approach is not unknown within traditional psychology. Science has been defined as "the game and art of describing a pattern within a system of sensing and conceptual... limits" (Agnew & Pike, 1969, p.174). Rogers's view of psychologists as pattern-perceivers is, then, to some extent accepted. It requires psychological researchers who are on intimate terms with the people they study. It requires researchers who, as personal construct psychologists have put it, maximize their interaction with the phenomena. How can such interaction be facilitated?

I can best answer this question by applying personal construct psychology to a range of areas of psychology. The areas I have selected are Physiological Psychology, Cognition and Perception, Learning, Personality and Individual Differences, and Social Psychology. This categorisation is not, of course, acceptable to personal construct psychology, which would not assume such a division into separate elements. It does, however, represent the typical approach of introductory textbooks in psychology and the thinking of many traditional psychologists (Toulmin, 1978). I shall address some of the same questions that psychologists who see themselves as working in these areas are themselves trying to answer. I have also chosen this mode of presentation because it enables me to show how methodology can develop as part of an approach to a problem. It need not be predetermined (Romanyshyn, 1971).

The sociophenomenological approaches in fact suggest no single paradigm for psychology (Keen, 1975). They prefer that psychologists should let their methods follow from the subject of their studies, the construing person (Spiegelberg, 1967). The more alternative perspectives through which we approach the person, the better (Kelly, 1955; Schütz, 1967). In Chapter 1, I posed a series of questions about the feasibility of these approaches that can now be answered. Is a science of the subjective interpretations of the construing person as viable as our traditional psychology of an alienated object? Can we identify our structures or patterns of interpretation in such a way as to establish intersubjective agreement? And, if we can, will they have bearing on the findings of traditional psychology? The answer to all three questions is, I believe: Yes.

Some part of what I have to say here is about the development of new procedures through a closer look at the assumptions which underlie the already established data collection methods of psychology. I shall also continue to be concerned, however, with possible modifications and amendments to old methods. For example, those established methods have tended to be predominantly quantitative while this personal construct psychology emphasis on interpretation requires that they be balanced by qualitative techniques (Filstead, 1981). Traditional psychology has produced useful enquiries which have provided people with much information about people. The logic of the traditional experiment remains of central importance to any science of psychology. As I have shown in Chapter 6, it is not my intention to discard or condemn established methods. I have suggested modifications for them, so that they can make their contribution to a psychology which is appropriate to the interpreting people who are its subject matter. In many cases the suggestions I make about how to tap into the experience of the co-researchers in one particular enquiry could well be implemented in other areas of psychology.

Physiological Psychology

Physiological psychologists may be said to concern themselves with two main questions. What are the relationships that can be established between physiological events and behaviour? And what are the relationships that can be established between physiological events and experience? The aim of one of the studies I described to illustrate the Experimenter Orientation Model in Chapter 2 was to relate the observed vigilance of co-researchers to a pattern of their concurrent cortical evoked potentials. The reference point beyond physiology was behaviour. That is, the study was intended to answer the first question, which does not focus on experience. I am no longer concerned with such studies in this volume. Other physiological studies have their reference points in experience, however. It is now appropriate to ask, in whose experience?

When these studies have invoked the Experimenter Orientation Model of data collection they have actually been studying the behaviours of co-researchers to the exclusion of their experiences. They have been concerned with their observed emotional states to the exclusion of their construed emotional states. They have examined the co-researchers' experiences as they are observed by the researcher. The procedures by which these psychologists collected information about the emotions of their co-researchers are primarily from outside them, as it were, through acts of the researcher (observations) rather than through acts of the co-researchers. The latter are rarely consulted as the centre of the experience of interest, and then only by rating scales formed, again, from the interpretations of the researchers.

The locus of experience can be properly returned to the subject of such studies in a variety of ways, but only if the researcher is prepared to trust the construing of co-researchers and their reports (Heron, 1981). Some psychologists are able to do this, for example, when content analysis scales are applied (Viney, 1983; Gottschalk, Lolas & Viney, 1986). Such an approach requires an increased emphasis on meaning. It also requires an acceptance of the co-researcher as a reflective knower, as having knowledge through experience and as being able to interpret, analyse and communicate this knowledge to others.

For example, co-researchers may be asked to talk of their experiences, as in Giorgi's (1975a) study of learning. Once a verbal report has been produced in this way, it can be approached using any of the descriptive procedures that have been discussed. The content can first be described and then examined for essentials, perhaps typical emotions in this case. An extension of the experiment might aim to relate the development of the experienced emotion of changing physiological events. Some traditional psychologists have already made use of dialogical phenomenology (Strasser, 1963) in their experimental procedure. When stooges approach the co-researchers of social psychological studies of emotion in their angry or euphoric moods, they are actually sharing

189

construed worlds. This is so even if the experience is not entirely authentic. Much more use of this technique can be made.

Now I shall turn to the interpretations of the researchers in such a study. They can be trained to relate to the co-researchers' construed world as well as they can, rather than interpreting the experimental events from their own perspective alone. If they are trained, they can produce much information that is relevant to any attempts to relate experience to other phenomena (Bannister, 1981). Their postexperimental debriefing of the co-researchers, for example, can become much more rewarding. They may come to collaborate with rather than manipulate their co-researchers. If their capacity for reflective knowing also becomes more appreciated, they can perhaps come to serve successfully as co-researchers of their own experiments. Useful studies involving the ingestion of certain drugs, for example, those with psychotomimetic properties, followed by careful self-monitoring of experience, have been carried out (Leary, 1968; Tart, 1971).

These suggestions are all appropriate for studies of experience. Where the interest is primarily in behaviour, as in the example of physiological psychology given in Chapter 2, there is no need for new data collection tools. If my aim is to observe the behaviour of another, I can do this within an "I-It" relationship, as described by Kaufman in his introduction to Buber's I and Thou (1970). The observed object is, essentially, an "It." If, however, I want to study the experience of another, I must do so in an "I-Thou" relationship. This is a relationship in which I am wholly committed and experiencing not just the particulars of an object but the whole "You" who are a construing person like me.

It is for this reason that psychologists maintain that the exclusively behavioural focus will not do for psychologists because they will, ultimately, seek to find the meaning of a person's behaviour in his or her construed world (Hudson, 1975; Apter, 1982; Murphy & Medin, 1985).

What new procedures, then, can be proposed for a physiological psychology which recognises itself as the study of interpreting people by interpreting people? The key appears to lie in the "I-Thou" relationship. Even though given the status of an "It," when linked physically to the necessary equipment, the co-researchers are still free to participate as "You" in interaction with the researcher. The researcher can create a dialogue with them through which their interpretations become accessible. They and the researcher can also role play together in such a way as to vary their emotional experience so that these variations can be related to variations in physiological events. Thus, if cause-and-effect relationships are sought, the experimental method can still be easily applied. We can also apply the techniques of social psychology and sociology (Schatzman & Strauss, 1973) to physiological studies. We can use our better developed (microchip-based) physiological instruments in field studies of people whose interpretations of their free-flowing experience can become available to psychologists. Then we should be able to identify naturally occurring patterns within and between the three domains of physiology, behaviour, and experience.

Finally, the approach of the ethnomethodologists, which was noted briefly in Chapter 5, can also be useful for this type of study (Garfinkel, 1967; Spradley, 1979). For our present purposes it can be applied to describe and analyse the ways in which researcher and co-researcher go about finding what they find in their enquiry (Hammersley & Atkinson, 1983). Garfinkel's focus has been on interpersonal interaction from which develops meaningful communication using symbols. The ethnomethodological and traditional psychological approaches differ in their interpretation of a psychological enquiry. Psychologists tend to devise their research to show, and therefore they find, generalisable, simple, and unambiguous results. In contrast, ethnomethodologists search for unique, rich, and often necessarily ambiguous outcomes. These differences occur because psychologists have tended to start with their own interpretations in the form of hypotheses. Ethnomethodologists, in the sociophenomenological tradition, eschew prior interpretations in favour of describing what they see as well as they can. Ethnomethodology has been used to describe the roles not only of the psychologist (Crowle, 1976) but of the subject (Psathas & Becker, 1972) and the experimenter (Turner, 1967) in psychological research.

Cognition and Perception

The question often asked by workers in the fields of cognition and perception is a different one. How do people relate to their worlds? Of course, there are different kinds of worlds. The psychophysical laws which have been derived have come mainly from the use of the Experimenter Orientation Model. They relate to a world representing physical entities, a world which is public to the extent that people seem to agree on what they perceive. One such law relates weight of objects as perceived by individuals to their weight as fixed by an agreed upon method of measurement. The Piaget-inspired study which I used to exemplify the Mutual Orientation Model, however, is concerned with a world of concepts, thoughts, ideas. Both worlds are psychological worlds, and so comprise construed experience. It is convenient, however, to view perceptual studies as concerned with how the co-researchers' world relates to the worlds of others, as represented by objective, or intersubjectively agreed upon, measurement. Cognitive studies can then be seen to be about how they order and make sense of that experience, or how they interpret it.

Even in studies of perception it is possible to use data collection models appropriate to construing people. Alapack (1971), for example, has studied the Mueller-Lyer illusion by presenting to co-researchers the simple line figure which appears in most introductory textbooks. When he had his co-researchers describe the figure he found that, although they perceived the line convergence which constitutes the illusion, that was only one of many perceptions. Information like this suggests that all experimental situations should be more carefully defined psychologically (Giorgi, 1970b). This description should be in words as well as numbers because words are the more effective symbols of psychological meaning. A more precise description of the relationship between co-researchers' interpretations of experimental situations and their interpretations of their construed worlds outside the laboratory is needed (Holland, 1977; Heron, 1981).

Psychologists have believed that tight control of researcher and co-researcher is necessary for intersubjectively agreed upon patterns in the relationships of the person to his or her perceived or cognised worlds to be identified. Phenomenology can make a contribution within these constraints (Scheerer, 1985). However, most studies of the concept of conservation do not fall within this tradition. What happens in such studies, when the researcher and co-researcher are free to explore the co-researcher's construed world, is that they both exert some controls of their own. This is because each is seeking to interpret the experience meaningfully. There are, rarely, irrelevant intrusions in the search for meaningful patterns by an involved researcher and a co-researcher whose curiosity has been stimulated. They may even perform their own hypothesis-testing experiments. Such an approach requires the full cooperation of co-researcher with researcher, and of researcher with co-researcher. The Mutual Orientation Model of data collection is aptly named.

In such a model, which recognises the active construing of the person, it is possible for co-researchers to serve as sources of hypotheses. They may also serve as checks on the experimental procedures and even as analysers of their shared data. Co-researchers may be asked to suggest what it might be in their construed worlds that they are attending to when they choose to perform certain acts. Hypotheses can in this way be born concerning, for example, determinants of cognition. They may also be asked for their particular perspective on certain aspects of the procedure of the experiment. Their experience as co-researchers makes possible a much less biased and, therefore, more rigorous check on the meaning of these procedures for other co-researchers, and whether this meaning is what the researcher intended. Even in a weight judgement study, this enlisting of the cooperation of the co-researcher can bring to light cues which co-researchers are using in their judgements other than those which the researcher has painstakingly manipulated. Finally, reflecting co-researchers can cast added light on their own behaviour by interpreting its meaning in the context of their experience, and so help in the analysis of their own data.

Such a view of the co-researcher's role in the study of cognition allows for a psychology between person and machine as well as for a psychology between people. It is the latter, however, with which we are concerned here, so we must look for more than interaction between "subjects" and computers, which present stimuli and analyse responses. In cognition, as well as in other areas of psychology, the interpretive abilities of the researcher are an important consideration. Those potential contributions of co-researchers which I have described can only be made if researchers are able to act in collaboration with them. In the Self-Orientation Model of data collection, for example, they cannot. The role of the researcher as a pattern perceiver is also particularly important here for perceiving the commonalities, consistencies, and structures in the ways in which people relate to their construed worlds. It is interesting to note in these modifications of the models of data collection originally presented that, regardless of their focus on cognition, the suggestions made are the same. Each suggestion involves people studying people and trying to make sense of their mutually construed world.

This holds true, too, when we look at a new means of working in these two not-so-different areas. It seems to me that Sardello's (1971) dialogue model can be useful here. An exploration of people's construed worlds within the framework of a free-flowing, interpersonal interaction is recommended. This exploration is reciprocal, each person in the dyad taking both co-researcher and researcher roles. One modification of the original method I would make is not to rule out the testing of hypotheses, as Sardello does. I believe, with Kelly, that people come to any experience with constructs, interpretations, or hypotheses which they naturally wish to test. The criterion by which results are judged is that

of intersubjective agreement, the criterion of any science. This would create an

objective meaning context of subjective meaning contexts (Schütz, 1967). This

use of the Mutual Orientation Model would also avoid disruptive hidden

dialogues between "experimenter" and "subject" and their all-too-frequent

alienation from each other.

Learning

Many of the suggestions for additions to the traditional paradigms made

above can be applied in the study of learning, which is, from a personal construct

perspective, the study of how people change. A valid and meaningful account of

the experience of change can be derived from co-researchers by researchers

who are trained to listen to them. Co-researchers can also provide hypotheses or

anticipatory interpretations, checks on procedures, and analyses of responses as

in other areas of psychology. Relatively little work has been concerned with

experienced learning, however. The focus of choice has been behaviour, often

behaviour conceived in stimulus-response terms. This has led to the

development of certain methods that are described chiefly in terms of the

behaviour of the experimenter (Stevens, 1935). One such method is the rote

learning method described in Chapter 2 as typifying the Self-Orientation Model.

This approach to the person through his or her behaviour is valid as faras

it goes. At the risk of being repetitive, I would remind you of the child learning a

new task whom I described at the beginning of this book. The external

observation of his performance produced a quite different view of learning from

that of his own experience. The former indicated that change occurred in the child; the latter located change in the task which was mastered. It is not, it seems, advisable to ignore the experience of learning to quite the extent that we have. In this context it is important to heed the reminders of the personal construct psychologists that no experiment, however carefully controlled, takes place in a vacuum. Both co-researcher and researcher are part of the Gestalt totality of that enquiry. And, to employ this notion of Gestalt further (Perls, Hefferline & Goodman, 1951), we must remember to study the Gestalt of the person in the total situation of the study of learning.

That Gestalt includes a view of co-researchers as reflective and active interpreters. They are capable of providing accounts of their own experience (Harré & Secord, 1972). This method of report involves asking co-researchers for their views of what interests the psychologist, even asking them to give their reasons for their behaviour. It provides information about how they wish to be seen by others (Harré, 1976). This is useful to the social psychologist; but is it useful to the psychologist whose focus is on learning? Armistead (1974) has shown that it can be by providing guidelines for the rigorous interpretation of such accounts. For example, their meanings should be established with several different readers or listeners. These meanings should be checked back with whoever gave the original account for validity. Any eventual classification should remain faithful to the original account so that predictions can be made on the basis of these classifications. These analytic steps are not unlike those taken by members of the Duquesne school of phenomenological psychology -- Giorgi, Colaizzi, Perrot and the Fischers -- in their examination of reports from co-researchers.

Careful control by the experimenters of experimental stimuli, in order eventually to be able to make statements about cause and effect, does not necessarily succeed.   In fact, the control of the stimuli belongs to the co-researcher who construes it (Landfield, 1976). Collaborating co-researchers are well able to exert controls, indeed to construct hypotheses-testing experiments, within the flow of their own experience. The parallel skills of researchers are important, too. The early work in Gestalt learning, even in apes (Kohler, 1956), testifies to this. That work required highly trained, empathic researchers; so it will be with some of the future developments in the area of learning.   Let us take, for example, that common ground of cognitive psychologists and learning psychologists -- memory -- as it was considered in that rote learning study of Chapter 2. What is memory if not construed experience of change?   And such construed experience can be tapped by a trained researcher providing a facilitating atmosphere of trust for his or her co-researcher.

Some of the most promising new approaches to the experience of learning have been those from the Duquesne school outlined in Chapter 3 (Giorgi, 1975a; Colaizzi, 1973). They reflected on descriptions of learning experiences which researchers elicited from one or more co-researchers. In all of these interactions, the ball was often in the co-researchers' court. They had, in other words, considerable control over how the data collection proceeded. They also worked with researchers whose main aim was to enable the co-researchers to communicate their experience meaningfully and, themselves, to meaningfully interpret that meaning. Power, then, was better balanced between co-researcher and researcher. Alienation between them was also minimised in these examples of the Mutual Orientation Model of data collection.

It is appropriate, too, to note that much broader definitions of learning are available within these less constricted approaches. I have been involved in a series of studies of learning in the form of reactions to crisis (Viney, 1976). Crisis is best described as a time of emotional upheaval. There are major changes in a person's lived world necessitating changes in the assumptions which he or she makes about it. Our studies of the emotional aspects of the crises of people who are hospitalised because of illness and of the beneficial effects of crisis intervention counselling provide relevant examples (Viney & Westbrook, 1982; Viney et al., 1985a & b). It is, incidentally, a further indictment of the artificial categorisation of psychology into subject areas that, while I have chosen to regard this research of my colleague and myself as learning research, it would often be classified under my next heading of "Personality." It will be, I believe, counterproductive for psychologists to restrict themselves to such categorisation in the future.

Personality and Individual Differences

Many different questions are asked under the heading of "Personality." One relatively simple question is this: What are the unique, identifying qualities of a person? Some developers of standardised tests of cognitive performance have chosen to answer this question in terms of the concept of intelligence, the value of which has turned out to be rather less than we had supposed. True, the tests have enabled us to make quantitative assessments of a very sophisticated type, but assessments of what? Perhaps the most useful definition of intelligence runs as follows: "Intelligence is the aggregate or global capacity of the individual to think rationally, act purposively, and deal effectively with his environment" (Wechsler, 1939, p.1). This conceptualisation makes clear that intelligence is closely akin to cognition because it involves an assessment of how efficiently a person relates to his or her world. It is not surprising, then, that the Mutual Orientation Model, used to elucidate -- as Piaget did -- the pattern of relationships which each person has with his or her world, is often employed in place of the only apparently rigorous measurement of the IQ.

The other main individual difference measures with which we are familiar have been designed to reveal other aspects of personality. The Eysenck Personality Inventory, one example of the Self-Orientation Model, claims to measure Neuroticism and Extroversion. We know that "subjects" react to standardised tests in a variety of different ways (Fiske, 1967). As a test, it takes no real account of the "subject's" experience. Its validity is demonstrated by empirical comparisons of scores of certain criterion groups of "subjects." Through it, then, it is very difficult to gain an impression of actively construing people, although it may assess some aspects of people's test-taking behaviour. The Rorschach Technique, however, aims to tap into their experience. It elicits the meanings objects have for them and so, if the symbolic interactionists are correct, points to how they may act. The Rorschach Technique, I have argued in Chapter 6, can be seen as an application of the Mutual Orientation Model.

Here are several more suggestions for the meaningful assessment of individual differences, following on those described in Chapter 6. More techniques that directly tap the interpreted experience of each individual must be developed. To do this, prior reconstruction of the co-researcher's construed world, as by standardised tests, should be minimised. Co-researchers should be able to express themselves from within their own construed worlds and not through that of someone else. The production of autobiography comes to mind here. We also have some special psychological techniques which are designed to achieve this expression, such as the Role Construct Repertory Technique and Self-Characterisation, but we need more. Research illustrating the role of language in the experience of self (Harré, 1976) and the assumptions depressives make in their lived worlds (Rowe, 1978) are exciting developments in this direction. They may indicate a growing interest among psychologists in meaning as well as measurement.

The case study is another useful technique which has been employed by psychologists for decades in order to learn about the unique qualities of the person (Rosenblatt & Kirk, 1982). Its focus on only one person has, however, been the reason for much criticism. That person has been viewed as a single data source providing no opportunities for comparisons. There is no reason, however, why data about one individual cannot be provided from different sources (Becker, 1970). For example, interaction with him or her in different situations may be fruitful. The logic of comparison which underlies the experimental method can be effectively applied in a case study (Campbell, 1979). It does, however, require sensitive, self-critical, reflecting researchers who test their interpretations or hypotheses carefully by making comparisons of many relevant instances from a range of data sources. In practical terms, this means that an historically accurate account of case analyses must be kept by researchers.

Exposure by reflecting people of their unique, identifying qualities is likely to be anxiety-arousing for them. It is important, therefore, that collections of this type of data should take place in the context of a supportive atmosphere provided by the researchers for the co-researchers. Further training of the researchers, perhaps in skills like the respect and accurate empathy taught to counsellors in training (Carkhuff, 1969), is necessary for even adequate use of the traditional individual difference paradigms.

The need for methods which are determined by their subject matter, rather than the availability of certain methods determining the aspects of the person to be studied, is apparent. They should be designed so as to aid in the emergence of a picture of the full person, the active chooser, interpreter, and reflector on his or her own experience. One set of methods has, indeed, led to such a picture of the person. I am thinking of Rogers's (1951) genuinely empathic and accepting approach to his clients, as the forerunner of Carkhuff's skills. These have given rise to exactly that picture of the person. This "I-Thou" dialogue of client-centred therapy, reminiscent of that advocated by Maslow for the relationship between the scientist and his or her subject of study, has demonstrated its capacity to enable a fuller image of the person to emerge.

Techniques which permit the natural development of a relationship between the researcher and the co-researcher appear to be particularly important in this bid to isolate the identifying characteristics of each person. For this reason, Mair devised his conversational model of interaction during the psychological enquiry. It is a relatively free-flowing reciprocal dialogue in which

202

each person takes responsibility for certain contributions, including information about himself or herself and reactions to information provided by the other person about himself or herself. By allowing the participants to choose to make either private or public statements, it recognises the right of the co-researcher to privacy (Mair, 1970). Because these conversations can continue over weeks or months, they provide an opportunity for the effects of both short- and long-term consequences of self-disclosure to become available and for the establishment of some patterns of change. The most striking feature of this application of the Mutual Orientation Model, however, is the way in which it exposes both participants to the possibility of change during the process of data collection. Too many data collections in the field of personality have ignored its dynamic quality, which has been well described and documented (Kelly, 1977).

Social Psychology

This model of data collection in which both the participants may change during their involvement in it is also much needed in Social Psychology. From the personal construct perspective, the main question posed by social psychologists is this: How do people relate to their social worlds? In other words, how do people interpret, organise, and choose between the interpersonal relationships which they see as being available to them? Of the studies outlined in Chapter 2, one Experimenter Orientation study was trying to answer that question in regard to initial impressions of others, while the Reactive Orientation Model study of attitude change was designed to elucidate how a person's social world could be influenced by the people in it.

How people form and organise their impressions of others, not only initial but lasting ones, remains something of a problem for psychologists. This is, of course, the problem which Kelly was addressing when he devised his Role Construct Repertory Technique. It was originally intended to clarify for the therapist the lived interpersonal world of the client in psychotherapy. The Technique, as can be seen in Chapter 6, is a device by which we may glimpse how other people construe their experience. In contrast, the method of the attitude change study is yet another which, while ostensibly concerned with experience, in fact has focussed on behaviour. The outcome of this study was again assessed in terms of responses on rating scales and observations of other behaviours of the "subjects" by the "experimenter." Not their construed experience, but the observed behaviour of the "subjects" was the focus.

In terms of suggested procedures for a Social Psychology one thing is clear. They can involve both "subject" and "experimenter" as people in a variety of interpersonal interactions. It is no longer viable to produce a psychology which is about the subjected "subject" only. New data collections can break with the old roles of "experimenter" and "subject" and so break with the old role expectations. One simple way to do this is to allow the co-researcher to ask the researcher questions. Let us imagine the effects on the results of that operant conditioning study of attitudes. The co-researcher asks: "Why do I have to give answers to these questions?" "Must I go on?" and "What is the purpose of all this?" If these questions had been answered by the researcher, an experimental situation closer to everyday life might have resulted. There might even have been less so-called attitude change. This revised procedure fits with the Mutual Orientation Model of data collection.

Another way in which the traditional role expectations for the science of psychology can be broken is by deliberately and systematically altering them, as in role play. To date it has been chiefly co-researchers who have been asked to play roles, for example, to pretend to have certain kinds of expectancies or lived worlds, while filling out personality inventories (Wales & Seeman, 1969). Researchers, too, can play roles in order to introduce new experimental conditions. Much can be learned, for example, from a role play by an adolescent researcher with an adolescent co-researcher about their representations of parental figures in their construed worlds. They can play the roles of parent and youth respectively from their own inner worlds and then reverse their roles while continuing their interaction. This procedure differs from the sociophenomenological view of everyday social interaction only in the concretisation or sharing of the steps toward mutual understanding. Soliloquies from these "characters" can also be enlightening. So can doubles for the characters played by other co-researchers, who can cast a new light on the role under study. This research methodology was born as a therapeutic strategy, in this case, psychodrama (Moreno, 1958), as were many such others. Such origins are not surprising, since psychotherapists have long been concerned with the construed experiences of their clients. If researchers and co-researchers can become spontaneously involved in their role play, as do the participants in psychodrama, a greater comprehension of interpreting people by interpreting people should result.

These procedures are examples of the techniques described more generally by Reason (1981). He, too, has assumed the study of interpersonal relationships to be concerned with the convergence of two flowing rivers of experience as two people relate to one another as interpreters and reflectors. He recognised that this assumption implies that he must deal with his subjects as responsible choosers. He has also accepted that, as an observer, he could not entirely grasp their experience nor focus on their relationship as they could. He resolved these problems by viewing the relating "subjects" he dealt with as researchers working towards a better understanding of their relationship, with himself in the role of facilitator. He gained from this technique rich, experience-based data which was embedded in the context of everyday life and yet of much relevance to social psychologists.

In Chapter 4 we learned something of the extent to which an "experimenter's" identity failed to become associated with the procedures of a psychological study. A valid psychology between construing people could not, then, emerge. There are, however, ways of doing psychological research, paradigms, if you like, which tend to be like those that were noted in Chapter 5. Action research (Sanford, 1970), for example, comes to mind as having possibilities in this respect. Bazeley (1978) employed this paradigm to enable her to study community development. She intervened experimentally in the development of the community of people she was studying. At the same time she attempted to monitor and assess some of the effects of her actions in terms of her predefined goal of better mental health for that community. She was a participant observer (Bruyn, 1966). She shared in the activities of the members of her community and became an accepted part of their culture. As she reflected on this, she found that her role came to reflect the social processes of that community. Participant observation is not only a tool for social psychologists. It can be applied to many other data collections as well.

There have been other developments in social psychology that are like participant observation in their emphasis on shared interpretations. They have differed in their intentions to replace, rather than add to, traditional experimental methods. Such systematic observation has, for example, become known as the dramaturgical method (Goffman, 1969). Each co-researcher's presentation of himself or herself is treated as if it were a theatrical performance. The actions of the co-researchers are explained by referring to their source in their intentions, for example, to guide the impression others have of them. As in the theatre, the scene, the actors in the scene, and the actions of the actors in the scene are taken into account by the psychologist who is trying to interpret them. Rule probing is another variant of this theme (Harré, 1974). Rules are construed patterns of social interaction which people choose to follow or not to follow. Observation of applications of these rules provides psychologists with important information about how people interact. It also provides information about the meaning of their actions in social situations (Marsh, Rosser & Harré, 1978). Scenarios, for example, can be presented to co-researchers to see how they apply the rules inherent in them. Rule probing helps to answer this question which social psychologists have been asking: How do people make sense of, organise, and choose interpersonal relationships? It is encouraging to note that at least one textbook on social psychology, with a sociophenomenological perspective, is available (Weigert, 1983).

Interpreting the Interpreters

These strategies for a science of construing people have been proposed under the fragmenting headings of the areas of traditional psychology. They may help to answer, however, a set of coherent and interrelated questions about interpreted experience. What are the unique, identifying properties of the experience of people? How do people relate to their physical worlds? How do people relate to their social worlds? How do people change? How are the domains of physiology and behaviour related to experience? The worlds referred to are personally interpreted worlds. Psychologists must gain access to them to answer the questions I have framed. They may not, of course, be questions of interest to all psychologists. Not all psychologists wish or need to study the construed experience of others. Yet, if we assume people to be active interpreters, we need to remember that the assumption applies to both our subjects and our experimenters or co-researchers and researchers, as well as to psychologists. The psychology that I have proposed is a psychology between people who are active decision makers, trying to make sense of their worlds, and able to reflect on and communicate about their own experience through the use of symbols.

The arena of research for this developing psychology is the experience and behaviour of people. The principles which govern the building up of its body of knowledge -- for example, the standards of reliability and validity applied to its assessment tools -- assume both psychologists and their subject matter to be interpreters. While subscribing to these principles, this psychology must also be related to the fruits of common sense. A psychology which recognises its own embeddedness in a construed world and that its so-called "facts" are socially created and interpersonally agreed on meanings, must protect itself from solipsism. Psychologists could easily agree among themselves on a view of "reality" which might prove to be in conflict with everyday experience (Wagner, 1974). Such conflict must be dealt with. Another possible trap for unwary practitioners of this relativistic form of science is the tendency to dualism (Evans, 1979). It is easier to overemphasise experience so as to detach it from behaviour than it is to maintain interpretations which integrate experience with behaviour.

My suggestions include a number of strategies for psychologists who are concerned with experience as well as behaviour. They require, as is now apparent from my examination of my own interpretations, that the psychologist examine his or her interpretations of the nature of psychological research and of the people who are part of it. They also enlist the aid of the cooperative co-researcher. They make the role of the researcher one which is more complex and requires more skill and, in fact, is much more important that it has been to date. When both co-researcher and researcher are free to relate in this Mutual Orientation Model of data collection there are likely to be fewer ethical problems. Further, the relationships within which data collection takes place should be helpful for both of the participants. They are more varied in nature, also, so as to provide a fuller and more generalised picture of the person.

This form of psychological research concerns itself with how the person relates to his or her construed world (Buytendijk, 1967). The psychologist focusses on how the co-researchers are aware of their situation, how they interpret it, what it means to them, and how they value it. Also, if psychology is the study of people by people, it will concern itself with the interpretations of the researcher. This psychology will include what I have to say about you and you about me. It is not only what is said about you and me by some anonymous third party. I have access to your observable behaviour but not to your construed experience, yet I need both to fully account for you. I, the researcher, need your cooperation as a co-researcher to relate construed experience to behaviour, the subjective perspective to the objective perspective. For people to study people only as objects is not sufficient (Lafitte, 1957).

Many criticisms will be levelled at this sociophenomenological approach. Inappropriate standards of objectivity will be required of it (Deutscher, 1983). It will be said that the assumptions that people construe, and the fact that the social and historical contexts affect their constructions, are irrelevant for much of psychology. It will also be argued that such assumptions undermine the search for consistencies in behaviour on which psychological laws are based. Such laws have most often been expressed in terms of physical properties, mechanics, and mathematical models and not in terms of people's interpretations. They have been verified through the logic of the experimental method, the controls for which are much harder to apply effectively with such people. It will be said that by including human experience in this psychology I have discarded all rational criteria for the acceptance or rejection of psychologists' interpretations, since there is no independent criterion of validity for assessments of "my experience." Not only have I questioned whether science can provide us with the truth about "reality," I have questioned whether there is one scientific method applicable to physical objects and human interpreters alike.

Many of the issues raised by this developing psychology remain unresolved. In my opinion, it is sufficient that the sociophenomenological approaches have heuristic value for psychologists. They have led and will continue to lead to alternative interpretations of human beings. Young children develop much of their early construct systems through interaction with the people who care for them. At first there is little common understanding. Gradually parent and child build up a set of agreed upon interpretations of their joint efforts to communicate (Tyler, 1981). This is how we can build up the more extensive construct system which will become our science of construing people.

References

Agnew, N. McK. & Pyke, S.W. (1969). The science game. Englewood Cliffs, New Jersey: Prentice-Hall.

Alapack, R.J. (1971). The physiognomy of the Mueller-Lyer figure. Journal of Phenomenological Psychology, 2, 27-47.

Apter, M.S. (1982). The experience of motivation. London: Academic Press.

Armistead, N. (1974). Reconstructing social psychology. London: Houghton Mifflin.

Ashworth, P. (1976). Some notes on phenomenological approaches in psychology. Bulletin of the British Psychological Society, 29, 363-368.

Bannister, D. (1981). Personal construct theory and research method. In P. Reason & J. Rowan (Eds.) Human inquiry (pp.61-70). Chichester: Wiley.

Bazeley, P. (1978). Community development for mental health. Unpublished doctoral thesis: Macquarie University, Sydney.

Becker, H.S. (1970). Sociological work. Chicago: Aldine.

Bruyn, S.T. (1966). The human perspective in sociology. Englewood Cliffs, New
Jersey: Prentice-Hall.

Buber, M. (1970). I and thou. (Translated by W. Kaufman) New York: Scribner.

Buytendijk, F.J.J. (1967). Husserl's phenomenology and its significance for
contemporary psychology. In N. Lawrence & D. O'Connor (Eds.)
Readings in existential phenomenology (pp.352-364). Englewood Cliffs,
New Jersey: Prentice-Hall.

Campbell, D.T. (1979). "Degrees of freedom" and the case study. In T.D. Cook &
C.S. Reichardt (Eds.) Qualitative and quantitative methods in evaluation
research (pp.110-122). Beverly Hills: Sage.

Carkhuff, R.R. (1969). Helping and human relations. New York: Holt, Rinehart &
Winston.

Colaizzi, P.F. (1973). Reflection and research in psychology: A
phenomenological study of learning. Dubuque, Iowa: Kendall Hunt.

Crowle, A.J. (1976). The deceptive language of the laboratory. In R. Harré (Ed.)
(pp.160-173). Life sentences: Aspects of the social role of language.
London: Wiley.

Deutscher, M. (1983). Subjecting and objecting: An essay on objectivity. St.
Lucia: University of Queensland Press.

Evans, C.S. (1979). Preserving the person. Madison, Wisconsin: Inter-Varsity
Press.

Farber, M. (1966). The aims of phenomenology. New York: Harper & Row.

Feyerabend, P. (1975). Against method. London: National Book League.

212

Filstead, W.J. (1979). Qualitative methods: A needed perspective in evaluation research. In T.D. Cook & C.S. Reichardt (Eds.) Qualitative and quantitative methods in evaluation research (pp.62-72). Beverly Hills: Sage.

Filstead, W.J. (1981). Using qualitative methods in evaluation research. Evaluation Review, 5, 259-268.

Fiske, D.W. (1967). The subject reacts to tests. American Psychologist, 22, 287-296.

Garfinkel, H. (1967). Studies in ethnomethodology. New York: Prentice-Hall.

Giorgi, A. (1970). Toward phenomenologically-based research in psychology. Journal of Phenomenological Psychology, 1, 75-98.

Giorgi, A. (1975a). An application of phenomenological method in psychology. In A. Giorgi, C.T. Fischer & E.L. Murray (Eds.) Duquesne Studies in Phenomenological Psychology. Pittsburgh, Pa.: Duquesne University Press, 2, 82-103.

Giorgi, A. (1975b). Convergences and divergences between phenomenological psychology and behaviourism: A beginning dialogue. Behaviourism, 3, 200-212.

Giorgi, A.; Barton, A. & Maes, C. (Eds.) (1983). Duquesne Studies in Phenomenological Psychology. Pittsburgh, Pa.: Duquesne University Press, 4.

Goffman, E. (1969). The presentation of self in everyday life. London: Penguin Press.

213

Gottschalk, L.A.; Lolas, F. & Viney, L.L. (1986). Content analysis of verbal behaviour in clinical medicine. Berlin: Springer Verlag.

Hammersley, M. & Atkinson, M. (1983). Ethnography: Principles and practice. London: Tavistock.

Harré, R. (1974). Blueprint for a study of science. In N. Armistead (Ed.) Reconstructing social psychology (pp.60-70). Middlesex: Penguin.

Harré, R. (Ed.) (1976). Life sentences: Aspects of the social role of language. London: Wiley.

Harré, R. & Secord, P.T. (1972). The explanation of social behaviour. Oxford: Blackwell.

Haworth, G.O. (1984). Social work research, practice and paradigms. Social Service Review, 59, 350.

Heineman, M.B. (1981). The obsolete scientific imperative in social work research. Social Service Review, 55, 371-397.

Heron, J. (1981). Philosophical bases for a new paradigm. In P. Reason & J. Rowan (Eds.) Human Inquiry (pp.110-121). Chichester: Wiley.

Holland, R. (1977). Self and social context. London: Methuen.

Hudson, L. (1975). Human beings. New York: Anchor.

Hyland, M.E. (1985). Do person variables exist in different ways? American Psychologist, 40, 1003-1010.

Imre, R.W. (1984). The nature of knowledge in social work. Social Work, 29, 41-45.

Keen, E. (1975). A primer in phenomenological psychology. New York: Holt, Rinehart & Winston.

Kelly, G.A. (1955). The psychology of personal constructs. New York: Norton.

Kelly, G.A. (1977). The psychology of the unknown. In D. Bannister (Ed.) New perspectives in personal construct theory. London: Academic Press.

Kohler, W. (1956). The mentality of apes. London: Routledge & Kegan Paul.

Kuhn, T. (1962). The structure of scientific revolutions. Chicago: University of Chicago Press.

Lafitte, P. (1957). The person in psychology: Reality or abstraction. London: Routledge & Kegan Paul.

Landfield, A.W. (1976). The interpretive man: The enlarged self-image. In A.W. Landfield (Ed.) Nebraska Symposium on Motivation, 24, 127-177.

Leary, T. (1968). The politics of ecstacy. New York: Putnam.

Mair, J.M.M. (1970). The person in psychology and psychotherapy: An Introduction. British Journal of Medical Psychology, 43, 197-205.

Marsh, P.; Rosser, E. & Harré, R. (1978). The rules of disorder. London: Routledge & Kegan Paul.

Mixon, D. (in press). On not doing and trying and failing. In A. Costall & A. Still (Eds.) Against cognitivism: Alternatives for a scientific psychology.

Moreno, J.; Moreno, Z. & Moreno, J. (1958). The discovery of the spontaneous man. New York: Beacon House.

Murphy, G.L. & Medin, D.L. (1985). The role of theories in conceptual coherence. Psychological Review, 92, 289-316.

Perls, F.S.; Hefferline, R.F. & Goodman, P. (1951). Gestalt therapy. Middlesex: Penguin.

Psathas, G. & Becker, P. (1968). The experimental reality: The cognitive style of a finite province of meaning. Journal of Phenomenological Psychology, 35, 500-520.

Reason, P. (1981). An exploration in the dialectics of two-person relationships. In P. Reason & J. Rowan (Eds.) Human Inquiry (pp.67-78). Chichester: Wiley.

Reason, P. & Rowan, S. (Eds.) (1981a). Human inquiry: A sourcebook of new paradigm research. Chichester: Wiley.

Reason, P. & Rowan, J. (1981b). Issues of validity in new paradigm research. In P. Reason & J. Rowan (Eds.) Human inquiry (pp.127-138). Chichester: Wiley.

Reinharz, S. (1979). On becoming a social scientist: From survey research and participant observation to experiential analysis. San Francisco: Jossey-Bass.

Rogers, C.R. (1951). Client centred therapy. Boston: Houghton Mifflin.

Rosenblatt, A. & Kirk, S.A. (1982). In defense of the case study method. American Journal of Orthopsychiatry, 52, 440-446.

Rowe, D. (1978). The experience of depression. New York: Wiley.

Salner, M. (1984). Needed: A human science for research in the helping professions. Smith College Studies in Social Work, 54, 95.

Sanford, N. (1970). Whatever happened to action research? Journal of Social Issues, 26, 3-24.

Sardello, R.J. (1971). A reciprocal participation model of experimentation. In A. Giorgi, W.F. Fisher & R. Von Eckartsberg (Eds.) Duquesne studies in phenomenology psychology. Pittsburgh, Pa.: Duquesne University Press, No.1, 58-65.

Schatzman, L. & Strauss, A.L. (1973). Field research: Strategies for a natural sociology. Englewood Cliffs, New Jersey: Prentice-Hall.

Scheerer, E. (1985). Edmund Husserl's phenomenology and contemporary cognitive psychology. Proceedings of the Founding Conference of the International Society for Theoretical Psychology. Plymouth: Plymouth Polytechnic.

Schütz, A. (1967). The phenomenology of the social world. Chicago: Northwestern University Press.

Scriven, M. (1969). Psychology without a paradigm. In L. Berger (Ed.) Clinical-cognitive psychology: Models and integrations (pp.9-24). Englewood Cliffs, New Jersey: Prentice-Hall.

Spiegelberg, H. (1967). The relevance of phenomenological philosophy for psychology. In E.N. Lee & M. Nandelbaum (Eds.) Phenomenology and existentialism (pp.219-241). Baltimore: Johns Hopkins.

Spradley, J.P. (1979). The ethnographic interview. New York: Holt, Rinehart & Winston.

Stevens, S.S. (1935). The operational definition of psychological concepts. Psychological Review, 42, 517-527.

Strasser, S. (1963). Phenomenology and the human sciences. Pittsburgh, Pa.: Duquesne University Press.

Tart, C. (1971). On being stoned. Palo Alto, Calif.: Science and Behaviour Books.

Toulmin, S. (1978). Wittgenstein: The Mozart of psychology. New York Review of Books, 25 (14).

Turner, R. (1967). The ethnology of the experiment. American Behavioural Scientist, 10, 8, 26.

Tyler, M. (1981). Kelly's 'road to freedom'? Problems in understanding the process of construct system development. In H. Bonarius, R. Holland & S. Rosenberg (Eds.) Personal construct psychology: Recent advances in theory and practice (pp.67-84). London: Macmillan.

Viney, L.L. (1976). The concept of crisis: A tool for clinical psychologists. Bulletin of the British Psychological Society, 29, 387-395.

Viney, L.L. (1983). The assessment of psychological states through content analysis of verbal communications. Psychological Bulletin, 94, 542-563.

Viney, L.L.; Clarke, A.M.; Bunn, T.A. & Benjamin, Y.N. (1985a). Crisis intervention counselling: An evaluation of long-term and short-term effects. Journal of Counselling Psychology, 32, 29-39.

Viney, L.L.; Clarke, A.M.; Bunn, T.A. & Benjamin, Y.N. (1985b). An evaluation of three crisis intervention counselling programmes for general hospital patients. British Journal of Medical Psychology, 58, 65-76.

Viney, L.L. & Westbrook, M.T. (1982). Patterns of anxiety in the chronically ill. British Journal of Medical Psychology, 55, 87-95.

Wagner, H.R. (Ed.) (1970). Alfred Schütz on phenomenology and social relations. Chicago: University of Chicago Press.

Wales, B. & Seeman, W. (1969). What do MMPI zero items really measure: An experimental investigation. Journal of Clinical Psychology, 4, 420-424.

Wechsler, D. (1939). The measurement of adult intelligence. Baltimore: Williams & Wilkins.

Weigert, A.J. (1983). Social psychology. Notre Dame: University of Notre Dame Press.

Wetherick, N.E. (1970). Can there be a non-phenomenological psychology? Journal of the British Society for Phenomenology, 1, 72-80.

INDEX

Assumptions, (cont'd)
    about the validity of different perspectives 5, 7
    and understanding of data 6, 165, 166
    author's 11, 17, 18, 151
    bracketing 8
    changes in, as a result of a crisis 198
    examination of, by psychologists 5, 11
    made by depressives 200
    of models of data collection 34, 36, 41, 47-50, 108, 118, 186
    of personal construct psychology 13, 66, 119
    of psychological research 120
    of social psychology 13
    of traditional psychologists 67, 75, 128
    phenomenologically based 71
    researcher's awareness of their own 5, 152
    underlying the psychology of personality 10
Atkinson, M. 191
Attribution theory research,
    and Mutual Orientation Model of data collection 160
    concerned with understanding interpretations 160, 161
    use of, to gain access to experience of co-researchers 155
Auden, W.H. 57
Australian Psychological Society 136

Bakan, D. 66
Baloff, N. 67
Bandura, A. 11
Bannister, D. 3, 67, 71, 88, 92, 107, 118, 128, 165, 168, 169, 170, 171, 189
Barber, T.X. 89, 94, 100, 101
Barry, K. 6
Barton, A. 185
Basic postulate,
    corollaries of 4
    of personal construct psychology 3
Baumrind, D. 136
Bazeley, P. 205
Becker, H.S. 200
Becker, S.W. 67, 191
Behaviour,
    affected by subjects 58, 195
    aggressive, personal construct psychology definition of 60
    and experience 14, 60, 62, 154, 187, 190, 193, 203, 208, 209
    and personal construct psychology 154, 195
    as focus of study of learning 195
    consistencies in 209
    directed towards an end 15-16
    interpersonal 120
    interpreted through communicative acts 16, 196

Data, (cont'd)
        psychological 18
        single person as source of 200
Data collection,
        and informed consent of subjects 44, 124, 135
        and interaction between experimenter and subjects 128, 130, 131, 136, 138, 172, 207, 208
        as a combination of observation and description 13
        as a series of interactions between researcher and co-researchers 132, 156, 158
        as an interaction between construing people 15, 19, 118, 120, 125, 139, 140, 154, 163, 166, 169, 172, 192, 203
        assumptions about humanity underlying 18, 118, 159, 186
        balance of power between subject and experimenter during 37, 38, 126, 133, 135, 139, 197
        by psychologists 15, 120, 131
        co-researcher's control over the process of 197
        deception as a source of error in 136
        demand characteristics of 12
        development of professional job role for 101
        development of role expectations during 125
        experience-based 72, 131, 139, 151, 152, 154, 159, 166, 187, 205
        in psychology as an interpersonal process 19, 44, 118, 119, 120, 121, 122, 123, 124, 130, 131, 132, 137, 140, 185
        limitations of, findings from 153
        models of, in psychology 31, 32, 38, 46, 60, 120, 126, 132, 134, 137, 139, 151, 153, 158-167, 172, 173, 183, 187, 192, 194, 202, 203
        new models of role of experimenter and subjects in 203
        reporting nature of research relationship during 138, 140, 172
        role of social psychologists in 120, 206
        role play, as a technique for 124, 204
        subject's concepts analysed in 45
        systematic bias in 64, 126
        tools of 3, 20, 140, 151, 152, 153, 154-164, 166, 167, 168, 169, 170-171, 173, 184, 189
        using a psychology of the co-researcher 137, 138, 198
        using computers 98, 108, 169, 194
        using content analysis scales 65, 103, 105, 161, 162
        using observed behaviour 187, 190, 205, 206
        using participant observation 205, 206
        using personality inventories 36, 70, 155
        using Role Construct Repertory Technique 168, 169, 170, 171, 172, 173
        using self-rating scales 156
Davis, K.E. 62
Davison, G.C. 162

Kelly, G.A. 3, 4, 12, 15, 55, 60, 70, 71, 74, 75, 90, 104, 129, 152, 159, 167, 168, 180, 186, 194, 202, 203
Kelman, H.C. 126, 136
Kendall, P.L. 156
Kendler, H.H. 164
Kirk, S.A. 200
Klett, C.J. 68
Knowledge,
     about construed worlds 8, 119
     about how experimenters affect subjects 100
     created by people 3
     distinction between experiential and observational 134
     gained through many perspectives 7, 183
Koch, S. 3
Kohler, W. 197
Koren, H.J. 130
Köstler, A. 67
Kotler, P. 98
Kuenzli, A.E. 56
Kuhn, T. 50, 183

Lafitte, P. 209
Laing, R.D. 19, 92, 134
Landfield, A.W. 55, 157, 197
Latchford, M. 121
Latour, B. 6
Lazlo, J.P. 62, 95
Lea, M. 171
Learning,
     after self-disclosure by experimenter 90
     and reflexivity 55, 88, 91
     as a partial process of psychology 130
     application of personal construct psychology in the study of 185, 195
     co-researchers' reports as data for study of 196
     different interpretations of 14, 195, 198
     Gestalt 197
     memory as common ground with study of cognition and 197
     phenomenological studies of 72
     studies of, in form of reactions to crisis 198
     studies of, using Reactive Orientation Model of data collection 42
     studies of, using Self-Orientation Model of data collection 29
     the study of, and the concept of Gestalt 196
     theory of hypnosis 56
Leary, T. 120, 189
Leenars, A.A. 171
Lefcourt, H.M. 96
Legan, D.R. 123
Lehman, R.S. 61, 122

Motives,
　　and experimenter bias 90
　　"because" types 16, 17, 58
　　during interpersonal interaction 17
　　"in order to" types 16, 17, 58, 90
　　interplay of 17
　　of experimenters 90, 107
　　reflexivity in accounting for 88
　　sharing of 17, 91, 107, 129
　　to engage in psychological research 69, 135
Murphy, G.L. 190
Musante, G. 62, 121
Mutual orientation,
　　and understanding of other's constructs 17
　　in a fully functioning interpersonal interaction 16-17, 31, 118
　　in a research relationship 96, 127, 129, 131, 134
　　in terms of symbolic interaction 90-91
Mutual Orientation Model of data collection,
　　and the concept of reliability 154, 165
　　and the concept of validity 154, 166, 167
　　and experience 152, 165, 167, 191, 199
　　and Role Construct Repertory Technique 153, 154, 172
　　and source of data 166
　　and Minnesota Multiphasic Personality Inventory 155
　　assumptions of 48, 49, 120, 153, 184
　　description of 32, 44, 73
　　ethics and use of 153, 208
　　experimenter's role in 32, 44, 46, 132, 203
　　mode of interaction between researcher and co-researchers (subjects)
　　132, 167, 172, 184, 193, 195, 198, 203, 208
　　stages of its communication process 153, 154, 156, 158, 159, 160, 161,
　　163, 164, 172, 173
　　subjects' role in 32, 44, 46, 132, 203
　　the Rorschach Technique as an application of 199
　　use of, in the assessment of intelligence 199
　　use of, in the replication of classical experiments 132
　　use of, in the study of perception and cognition 191-195, 199
　　use of, in the study of personality 202
Myths,
　　interpreters, as makers of 99, 108
　　perpetuated by computers 98
　　the making of, as a way of construing experience 92

Nelson, T.M. 135
Nicholson, M. 165
Neimeyer, R.A. 169
Nisbett, R.E. 152
Norman, D.A. 98

Stringer, P. 118
Subject error,
     as an integral part of the person 68, 89, 100
     studies of 69
     view of traditional psychologists about 68, 135
Subjectivity,
     and personal construct psychology 137, 154
     and phenomenological psychology 9, 10
     as ground for objectivity 9, 119, 195, 209
     concern of psychologists about 8
     interpersonal, as an integral part of psychology 119, 131, 185, 195
Subjects,
     accounts of their behaviour and reflexivity 88, 89
     alienation of, by psychologists 125, 127, 135, 139, 171, 186, 195, 198
     and ethical issues in research 58, 68, 136
     and experimenters, balance of power between 37, 38, 67, 97, 125, 126, 133, 139, 140
     and experimenters, cooperation between 59, 69, 72, 73, 75, 104, 107, 127, 132, 139
     and experimenters, dialogue between 129, 133, 135, 139, 190, 195, 201
     and experimenters, interaction between 20, 32, 39, 40, 41, 44, 50, 67, 98, 102, 106, 118-127, 130, 134, 135, 137, 139, 151
     as active choosers 46, 54, 59, 64, 75, 135, 205
     as actors 128
     as construing people 20, 39, 40, 46, 50, 54, 58, 60, 62, 68, 69, 71, 75, 107, 119, 122, 126, 129, 131, 135, 139, 203
     as co-researchers 131, 133, 134, 137, 138, 139
     as creators of meaning 46, 60, 124, 125, 129, 138
     as data analysts 73
     as individuals and groups 32
     as makers of interpretations 54, 58, 62, 66, 69, 75, 104, 122, 123, 125, 128, 151, 208
     as objects 57, 209
     as organisers of their experience 60, 102, 199, 200
     as reflective knowers 54, 63, 65, 75, 124, 131, 151
     as source of hypotheses 74, 193, 195
     assumption about in psychology 67
     author's assumptions about 4, 17, 18, 57, 74, 75
     communication with, by experimenters 41, 91, 95, 102, 124, 138, 151
     construing of, by psychologists 37
     deception of 63, 68, 124, 128, 137, 139
     definition of stimuli to which they are to respond 57, 139
     effects of experimenters on 100, 120-122
     effects of their suspiciousness 63, 75
     effects of, when apprehensive 59, 63, 75
     expectations of 61, 64, 95, 120, 122, 125
     experimenters as, in their own research 103, 104, 106
     experimenters' views of 11, 54, 57, 58, 60

Taylor, S.J. 102
Teilhard de Chardin, P. 7
Thomason, B. 15
Titchener, E. 66
Tolman, E. 55, 66, 119
Toulmin, S. 105, 185
Turner, R. 128, 191
Tych, A.M. 65
Tyler, D.M. 122
Tyler, M. 210

Unger, R.K. 6

Validity,
    and personal construct psychology 167
    concurrent 167
    construct 92, 166, 167, 170, 171
    content 155, 160, 170
    criteria of, for experience-based data collection 152, 167, 171
    criterion 166-168, 199
    in relation to the method of data collection 167, 171, 173
    of assessments of experience 166, 209
    of different perspectives 5
    of interpretations 125, 128, 196, 207
    of psychological tools of data collection 164
    of results 133
    of Role Construct Repertory Technique 170, 171
    of scores on content analysis scales 162
    predictive 167, 168, 171
    standards of 154, 164, 207
    traditional definition 164
Van de Riet, V. 123
Van Hoose, T. 59
Van Kaam, A. 3
Verbal reports,
    content analysis of 161
Vigilance,
    task and Experimenter Orientation Model of data collection 40, 187
Viney, L.L. 65, 68, 73, 94, 96, 99, 103, 162, 163, 188, 198
Von Eckartsberg, R. 134

Waag, W.L. 122
Wagner, H.R. 19, 208
Wales,R. 204
Walster, E. 12, 129
Watzlawick, P. 7
Webb, W.B. 90
Weber, S.J. 59

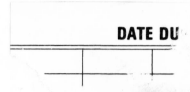

DATE DU